Exploring Nature with Your Child

By the Editors of Time-Life Books

Alexandria, Virginia

TIME ®
LIFE
BOOKS

Time-Life Books Inc.
is a wholly owned subsidiary of

Time Incorporated

FOUNDER: Henry R. Luce 1898-1967

Editor-in-Chief: Jason McManus
Chairman and Chief Executive Officer:
J. Richard Munro
President and Chief Operating Officer:
N. J. Nicholas, Jr.
Editorial Director: Ray Cave
Executive Vice President, Books: Kelso F. Sutton
Vice President, Books: George Artandi

Time-Life Books Inc.

EDITOR: George Constable
Executive Editor: Ellen Phillips
Director of Design: Louis Klein
Director of Editorial Resources: Phyllis K. Wise
Editorial Board: Russell B. Adams, Jr., Dale M.
Brown, Roberta Conlan, Thomas H. Flaherty, Lee
Hassig, Donia Ann Steele, Rosalind Stubenberg,
Henry Woodhead
Director of Photography and Research:
John Conrad Weiser
Assistant Director of Editorial Resources:
Elise Ritter Gibson

PRESIDENT: Christopher T. Linen
Chief Operating Officer: John M. Fahey, Jr.
Senior Vice Presidents: Robert M. DeSena, James L.
Mercer, Paul R. Stewart
Vice Presidents: Stephen L. Bair, Ralph J. Cuomo,
Neal Goff, Stephen L. Goldstein, Juanita T. James,
Hallett Johnson III, Carol Kaplan, Susan J.
Maruyama, Robert H. Smith, Joseph J. Ward
Director of Production Services:
Robert J. Passantino

Library of Congress Cataloging-in-Publication Data
Exploring nature with your child.
   (Successful parenting)
   Bibliography: p.
   Includes index.
   1. Nature study. 2. Parent and child.
I. Time-Life Books.   II. Series.
QH51.E97 1988   508   88-2229
ISBN 0-8094-5950-7
ISBN 0-8094-5951-5 (LSB)

Successful Parenting

SERIES DIRECTOR: Dale M. Brown
Series Administrator: Jane Edwin
Editorial Staff for *Exploring Nature:*
Designer: Raymond Ripper
Picture Editor: Marion F. Briggs
Text Editors: Margery A. duMond, John Newton,
Moira J. Saucer
Researchers: Sydney Johnson, Karin Kinney,
Patricia N. McKinney, Fran Moshos
Assistant Designer: Cynthia S. Capozzolo
Copy Coordinators: Marfé Ferguson, Charles
J. Hagner
Picture Coordinators: Betty Weatherley,
Linda Yates
Editorial Assistant: Jayne A. L. Dover

Special Contributors: Amy Aldrich, Dónal Kevin
Gordon, Susan Perry (text); Anne Muñoz-Furlong,
Julie Trudeau (research); Louise Hedberg (index)

Editorial Operations
Copy Chief: Diane Ullius
Production: Celia Beattie
Library: Louise D. Forstall

Correspondents: Elisabeth Kraemer-Singh (Bonn);
Maria Vincenza Aloisi (Paris); Ann Natanson
(Rome)

First printing. Printed in U.S.A.

Published simultaneously in Canada.
School and library distribution by
Silver Burdett Company, Morristown, New Jersey
07960.

TIME-LIFE is a trademark of Time Incorporated
U.S.A.

Other Publications:

THE TIME-LIFE GARDENER'S GUIDE
MYSTERIES OF THE UNKNOWN
TIME FRAME
FIX IT YOURSELF
FITNESS, HEALTH & NUTRITION
HEALTHY HOME COOKING
UNDERSTANDING COMPUTERS
LIBRARY OF NATIONS
THE ENCHANTED WORLD
THE KODAK LIBRARY OF CREATIVE
   PHOTOGRAPHY
GREAT MEALS IN MINUTES
THE CIVIL WAR
PLANET EARTH
COLLECTOR'S LIBRARY OF THE CIVIL WAR
THE EPIC OF FLIGHT
THE GOOD COOK
WORLD WAR II
HOME REPAIR AND IMPROVEMENT
THE OLD WEST

*For information on and a full description of any
of the Time-Life Books series listed above, please
call 1-800-621-7026 or write:*
Reader Information
Time-Life Customer Service
P.O. Box C-32068
Richmond, Virginia 23261-2068

This volume is one of a series about raising children.

The Consultants

General Consultant

Thomas D. Mullin, the overall consultant for this book, is a naturalist who specializes in developing and promoting conservation lectures, nature walks, animal habitat studies, and other similar park programs and exhibits for the education and enjoyment of both children and adults. He is Director of the Hidden Oaks Nature Center, a part of Virginia's Fairfax County Park Authority. Mr. Mullin is a former board member and an active participant in the National Association of Interpretation, a professional organization of natural and cultural history interpreters; for several years, he has presented many of his innovative programs at its national and regional workshops. He is also on the advisory committee for the Natural History Field Studies and Horticultural Program, an adult education program sponsored by the U.S. Department of Agriculture for professional and amateur horticulturists.

Special Consultants

Howard W. Boyd contributed the expert's box on camp for preschool children *(page 129).* With his wife, Betty, he is codirector, as well as general manager, of Gwynn Valley, a summer camp for boys and girls aged five to twelve that was founded in North Carolina in 1935. Mr. Boyd, who was certified as a camp director by the American Camping Association in 1975, has been actively involved with Gwynn Valley for twenty-one years.

Dr. Ronald Moglia, a recognized authority on human sexuality, provided advice for the essay *Telling the Story of Life* on pages 40-47 and presented his views on discussing sex with children in the expert's box on page 41. As Professor and Director of the Human Sexuality Program in the Department of Health Education at New York University, he teaches and conducts research, including studies on the sexual development of children. Dr. Moglia is a consultant to schools and health organizations and is the author of more than twenty publications dealing with human sexuality, including *On the Road to Good Family Life and Sexual Health,* the first kindergarten-to-third-grade curriculum guide based on children's developmental learning. Among his professional affiliations are the Society for the Scientific Study of Sex and the American Association of Sex Educators, Counselors and Therapists.

Dr. Judith A. Schickedanz, a child-development specialist, was the consultant for the first two sections of this book. She is an associate professor in the Department of Early Childhood Education and head of the Early Childhood Learning Laboratory, an innovative program for preschool children, both at the Boston University School of Education. Her published titles include *Toward Understanding Children* and *Strategies for Teaching Young Children.* She has also generated many scholarly articles and presentations on concept development in children and the role of play in early childhood learning processes. She is an active member of the National Association for the Education of Young Children and other professional organizations.

Karen Travers, Programs Coordinator for the Delaware Nature Society, contributed to the fourth section of this book, on wilderness trips with your children. She plans and supervises more than 200 programs a year for the society, focusing on environmental education and the protection of natural areas, and conducts nature study trips in the United States and abroad. Ms. Travers has taught field biology and environmental science to children and adults, consults for several school districts on their environmental-science curriculum, and is a director of the Delaware Association of Biology Teachers and president of the Mid-Atlantic Marine Education Association.

Contents

3

Where the Wild Things Are   76

4

The Joys of Family Camping   110

Child of Nature

You are no doubt always looking for activities that will interest your child and pique his curiosity. What better place to look than outside, where nature awaits? Dynamic and ever-changing, with unlimited potential for exploration, this world of weather, plants, animals, and insects, with its endless cycles of birth and growth, is the perfect adventureland for children—and it presents wonderful opportunities for family fun, too.

The text that follows will help you introduce your child to this vibrant world. You do not have to be a nature expert to get started. Your child is a natural explorer; you need stay only one step ahead of him. You can awaken his sense of wonder, for example, simply by providing new experiences for him, as the grandmother holding up her granddaughter to touch and smell a rose is doing at right. You will find abundant opportunities in your home environment, in the form of a purring kitten, a passing bee or butterfly in the garden, a spider in the tool shed, or a robin tussling with an earthworm on the lawn. For a two-year-old, the habits of these creatures may seem sheer magic, but as he grows, so will his understanding and interest. Soon, he may be ready to try some of the projects in this chapter, perhaps raising a caterpillar into a butterfly, or planting a seed and nurturing it into a blossoming plant, or keeping a chart of the daily weather. Or he may enjoy more structured activities, such as trips to the zoo or botanical garden, or even a family overnight outing at a campsite in the woods.

As you and your child explore nature, you may discover that he is benefiting in unforeseen ways that go beyond mere amusement and learning, beyond even the binding joy of shared adventures and discoveries. You may find that his child's world view has expanded beyond self and family to a larger family that includes all living things—the beginnings, perhaps, of a philosophical attitude that will sustain him all his days.

An Adventureland at Your Doorstep

Nature's wonders are not confined to exotic, faraway lands, especially in the eyes of small children. Chances are, your youngster will be just as thrilled by the sight of a sparrow or squirrel on your windowsill as she would be by the sight of a bald eagle in Alaska or an elephant in Africa. Indeed, for her, every discovery, no matter how trivial it might seem to you, can be the occasion for wide-eyed wonder.

Sharing these simple experiences with her will be a source of great pleasure for both of you, and it will give you a chance to rekindle your own interest in nature and see your surroundings with fresh eyes. Your garden, a nearby park, even a vacant city lot abound with opportunities for potential discoveries. City children and country children alike can find much to marvel at in the growth of plants and the behavior of pets, in the changes of seasons, in the starlit canopy of the sky, and in the daily whims of the weather.

A special sense of wonder

Now is the time to nourish your child's zest for living. The same innate curiosity that lends magic to her playtime also lights the path to the world of nature. So much is new to her now, and there is so much to learn, that she brings to each encounter an infectious sense of wonder that can generate new enthusiasms and interests and become the basis for a close and deep relationship with the environment. Under your guidance and gentle encouragement, she will soon learn that each and every living thing has its place in the world and that each deserves its own measure of respect.

Your role as guide

Introducing your child to nature need not require any special planning, since daily life presents plenty of opportunities to take note of passing birds, animals, and insects or to explain to her that your favorite houseplant needs water and food just as she does. Later, as she grows and her awareness of the world around her increases, you may want to devote more time to more structured activities, including bird watching, simple science experiments, and nature walks in a local park or woodland.

Whatever the activity, keep in mind that in serving as a guide to your child's sometimes puzzling surroundings, you do not want to overwhelm her. Problems may start if you try to push her in a direction that she does not want to go. Make it your goal to help her pursue her own special interests. Above all, you want to stimulate her own powers of observation and reasoning. Whenever you can, use questions and suggestions to help her draw her own conclusions. Plan, then, to have a committed but subtle role in your youngster's nature experience. You will be bombarded with questions, of course, but do not expect to know all the answers. Incessant as they may be, your child's frequent "whys" and "hows" are not meant to trigger an encyclopedic rundown of facts. Besides, you can always find out the answers together, a wonderful first step toward learning.

A boy uses a chart to identify two birds feeding on the seeds he set out for them in a backyard bird feeder. Installing a feeder is only one of many ways to engage a child in the living world around him.

Use all the senses

Observing nature involves more than just looking. You should make every effort to encourage your child to use all of her senses—not only to see, but to listen, to smell, and whenever safe and appropriate, to taste and to touch. In doing so, your young explorer will gather even more information about a particular outdoor discovery or natural phenomenon and can then use that information to move from curiosity to inquiry to understanding.

The accessibility of nature

As you and your youngster set out to explore the world of nature, keep in mind that nature is all around you; the only barriers to discovery are those you erect yourself. Begin, then, by looking close to home. If, like many families, you keep a pet, encourage your child to observe the animal and apply what she learns to the wider world of wilder animals. Together, you and your little one can also grow plants from seeds or watch a bulb explode in a riot of color and perfume—experiences with lessons for your inquisitive child. Even more surprises await you outdoors. You have only to take your little one by the hand and begin. ⁖

Learning from Pets

You can be sure that looking at pictures of animals, listening to stories about them, and watching nature programs on television are all good for your growing child, but there is nothing to beat the experience of actually having one or two animals of his own. He needs to pet and handle living creatures, to listen and talk to them, and even to care for them on a day-to-day basis. By getting to know them this way, he can begin to understand how uniquely different they are and so gain an insight into their lives. And that understanding will not only lay the foundation for a healthy respect for the animal kingdom but will also ward off any fears or misconceptions he might otherwise develop about certain creatures and their behavior.

All this can best be accomplished at home, provided, of course, that you are comfortable with animals yourself and are willing to devote the time, money, and effort required to care for a pet properly. You may find the investment well worth your while; as a source of day-in, day-out interest, few toys can compete with a good pet for a child's attention.

The family pet can help your little one develop a number of simple concepts. In caring for a pet, he will learn that animals need food, water, space, and shelter just as people do. And even though most of today's pets were domesticated long ago, they display behavioral traits inherited from their wild ancestors. Watching a cat stalk a mouse, for example, your child can readily imagine a tiger on the prowl.

Understanding an animal's behavior will help a child avoid unnecessary bites and scratches. For this reason, show your youngster your dog's teeth (above) and point out that it will bare them when frightened or angry. Also show how the family cat, under similar circumstances, will straighten its toes to unsheathe needle-sharp claws (below, right).

The specialness of cats and dogs

Your child's first encounter with animals is likely to come in the form of a friendly dog or cat and is just as likely to be a hands-on experience as he playfully touches it. Such moments lend themselves to lessons in "petiquette" *(page 13),* involving the proper way to treat animals, as well as to further explorations under your supervision. If he is very young, you might stimulate his interest further by asking him to look closely at the cat's ears or to tell you how many legs the dog has.

You can pique an older preschooler's interest by calling attention to the characteristics that make dogs and cats special. For example, both animals hear far better than people do. At the sound of a shrill whistle, your dog or cat may perk up uncomfortably or even leave the room. You can explain that sounds that are acceptable to humans can be objectionable to the animal's ultrasensitive ears. You might also point out that while dogs and cats see well in dim light, they cannot see colors. Or that both animals have highly developed senses of smell. In fact, a dog's world centers on its nose, which it uses to sift through a plethora of scents—something worth noting as your youngster gleefully watches Fido sniff excitedly through a pile of leaves in search of a lost ball. You can point out that a cat's whiskers are not just long hairs, but valuable sense organs that allow the animal to judge the width of an opening before squeezing through. And any child will be delighted to know that the family dog regards him as a member of its pack, or that when his cat rubs against him, it is marking him with its personal scent—a signal to other cats that this boy belongs to this kitty.

Caring for dogs and cats

Dogs and cats require a degree of responsibility that is beyond the maturity level of most preschoolers. Nonetheless, it is a good idea to involve your child in some aspect of the pet's feeding, grooming, or

exercising. Even a three-year-old can hold a food or water bowl while you fill it, and she may delight in serving the animal herself. Such participation helps her to understand that tame animals are dependent on people. She may also enjoy knowing that, just as she must pay regular visits to a doctor for checkups, so too must her dog or cat—which has a special doctor of its own.

Small mammals By virtue of their confinement in cages, gerbils, white mice, and guinea pigs are good subjects for the study and appreciation of smaller creatures. Most children love to watch their pets put exercise wheels and small toys to noisy use. Another welcome attribute of these small pets is that their needs are few: They require only a clean cage in a draft-free location, adequate food, and water. With supervision, an older preschooler may be able to look after them himself. Less welcome, however, is the fact that most rodents bite and rarely take kindly to handling. They are also prolific breeders.

Fish as pets Most children enjoy watching fish dart this way and that and then pause, seemingly motionless, in a bowl or aquarium. You can point out that most species are equipped with a special organ called a swim bladder, which allows them to remain still without sinking in the water. Although fish have no ears, some, such as goldfish, can feel sounds through their skin. Your youngster may be relieved to know that her apparently tireless fish do indeed sleep—but with eyes wide open since they have no eyelids. And should she ask why her fish are forever gulping water, you can explain that this is how they breathe. Tell her that the fish's gills, located inside the flaps on both sides of its head, extract air from the surrounding water.

Caring for fish Goldfish require no special equipment. A bowl of room-temperature water is all that is necessary to get started. You will need to

Caring for fish and birds requires special skills children can acquire. The little girl below has learned not to startle her parakeet as it perches trustingly on the side of a glass to sip water. The boy at above right is being careful not to overfeed his goldfish. Excess food will fall to the bottom and encourage the growth of harmful bacteria.

change the water every two to three days, but make sure to draw it from the tap a day in advance to allow any potentially deadly chlorine to dissipate and the water to warm to room temperature. Feed the fish twice a day, giving them only as much flaked fish food as they eat in two or three minutes' time.

Tropical fish require a greater financial commitment. To raise them successfully, you will need an aquarium, a heater to maintain the water temperature, and a pump and filter to keep the water aerated. Your pet shop can recommend species that are compatible with one another and advise you on how to care for them properly.

Birds Choosing a bird is a simple matter of deciding what kind to buy and then going to a reputable pet shop or breeder. The seller can advise you on care requirements and the type of cage to buy. An older preschooler may take special pride in being trusted to keep the pet's seed and water cups full.

Parakeets are particular favorites with children because they are trainable. Some can learn to perch on a finger and others will push marbles or small balls about with their bills. Best of all, parakeets are capable of mimicking speech. The skill is an acquired one; the birds merely repeat sounds that they hear and will just as readily bark like a dog as say hello. If your parakeet shows an interest in talking, encourage it by repeating a word or phrase whenever you are near its cage. Placing a tape recorder nearby, with a recording that repeats one word over and over again, is another effective training device. Be patient, and in time your efforts may be rewarded. But do not be disappointed if your bird is content with the natural chirping and twittering of its species.

If singing is more to your liking, consider buying a canary. Unlike the parakeet's talking, the canary's singing is an inherited skill. Male canaries sing better than females—a mating trait left over from their natural state in the wild. They can add a note of sunny cheer to a home and become, through their playful song, regular members of the family. ❖

The Dos and Don'ts of "Petiquette"

- Give your pet lots of love and attention. Animals thrive on it.
- Avoid hurting an animal in any way.
- Never bother a dog or cat, especially while it is eating.
- Do not try to grab anything from your pet's mouth.
- Try not to startle your dog or cat.
- Never hold a dog or cat by its neck or legs, or pick up a rabbit by its ears.
- Never disturb a mother animal and its young.
- Handle rodents carefully. They are liable to bite.
- Never tease your pet, even good-naturedly.

Fun with Indoor Plants

Although plants may lack the appeal of a house pet that can fetch, purr, or scamper around an exercise wheel, they, too, are living things, with a magic of their own. Under your guidance your youngster will soon come to appreciate the special nature of indoor plants and experience the fun and self-satisfaction that comes from planting a seed, nurturing it, and watching it grow.

Indoor gardening need not be an elaborate affair; indeed, it can be as simple as dropping a few pumpkin seeds into a plastic egg carton full of soil or growing alfalfa sprouts on a dampened paper towel. But even on the smallest scale, indoor gardening can serve as a first step in understanding a number of important facts about plant growth. As you teach your little one to plant seeds, for example, you can explain that seeds are storehouses of life and that inside each seed's protective outer coat lies an embryo plant complete with the food supply it needs to sprout and develop.

Eventually, your child will come to understand that there are many kinds of seeds—from the light downy seed of a dandelion to the hard round nut of an acorn—and that under the right conditions, any seed can sprout and grow into a new plant. She will also learn that there are many kinds of plants and that flowers, leaves, bulbs, stems, fruits, and roots are among the special names given to the various parts of each. Sometimes these parts can even be used to grow a new plant. To demonstrate that fact, simply cut the top inch off a carrot and place it in a jar lid that you have filled with water. Providing you take pains to replenish the water when it runs low, tiny roots will appear on the cut edge of the carrot within a few days, while feathery shoots will begin sprouting from the top.

On this and the following pages you will find several projects designed to introduce your youngster to the pleasures of indoor planting. They will give her the chance to grow plants not only from seed, but also from bulbs, tubers, and cuttings. She can even grow her own mold garden (page 17)—but before you begin this project, be certain she has no mold allergies. Although all of these activities are child-size, you will need to match the task to your child's skills. Older children will be able to do many of the projects on their own, but a younger child will need your help, since her little fingers may not be adept enough to plant tiny seeds successfully or to water them without drowning the tender new roots in the process.

A sponge garden grown from seed

A household sponge is an ideal medium for growing a minigarden. Use grass seed or birdseed that has been soaked in water overnight. Wet the sponge and place it in a dish, then sprinkle the seed on top and set the dish in a sunny spot. Be sure to keep the sponge moist.

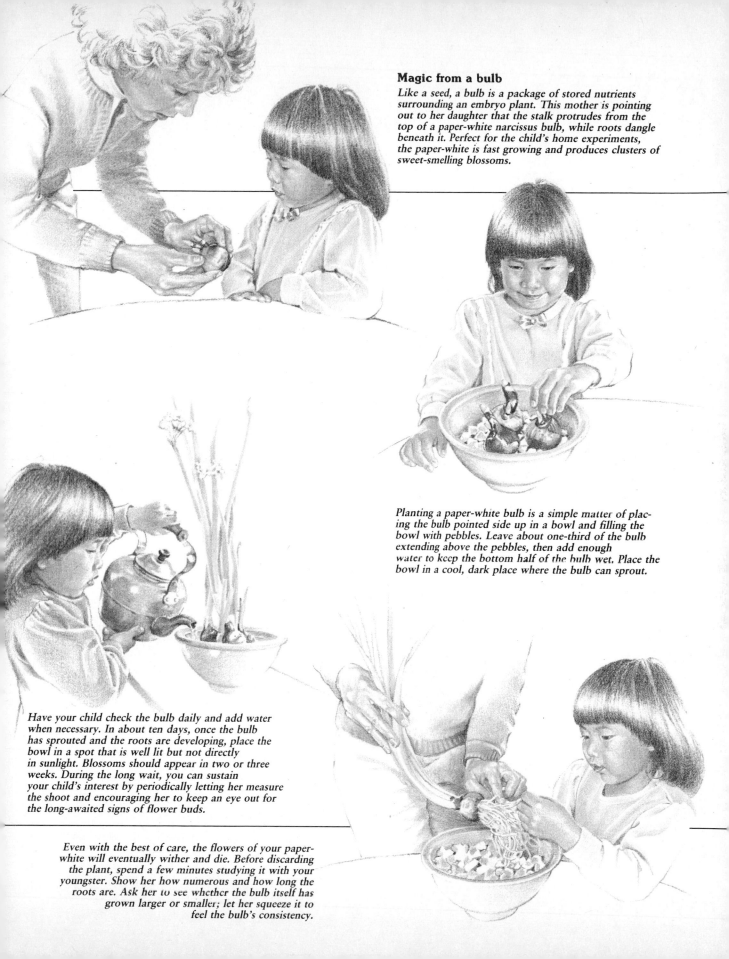

Magic from a bulb

Like a seed, a bulb is a package of stored nutrients surrounding an embryo plant. This mother is pointing out to her daughter that the stalk protrudes from the top of a paper-white narcissus bulb, while roots dangle beneath it. Perfect for the child's home experiments, the paper-white is fast growing and produces clusters of sweet-smelling blossoms.

Planting a paper-white bulb is a simple matter of placing the bulb pointed side up in a bowl and filling the bowl with pebbles. Leave about one-third of the bulb extending above the pebbles, then add enough water to keep the bottom half of the bulb wet. Place the bowl in a cool, dark place where the bulb can sprout.

Have your child check the bulb daily and add water when necessary. In about ten days, once the bulb has sprouted and the roots are developing, place the bowl in a spot that is well lit but not directly in sunlight. Blossoms should appear in two or three weeks. During the long wait, you can sustain your child's interest by periodically letting her measure the shoot and encouraging her to keep an eye out for the long-awaited signs of flower buds.

Even with the best of care, the flowers of your paper-white will eventually wither and die. Before discarding the plant, spend a few minutes studying it with your youngster. Show her how numerous and how long the roots are. Ask her to see whether the bulb itself has grown larger or smaller; let her squeeze it to feel the bulb's consistency.

A new plant from a single stem

*Begonias and many other flowers can grow new plants
from leaf or stem cuttings. To see how, first prepare a
rooting medium by placing a layer of pebbles in the
bottom of a small pot and covering it with a layer of
sand and a third layer of sphagnum moss. Wet the
medium and wait a few minutes for the water to be
absorbed. Then, using your finger, make a hole in the
medium and insert a leaf or stem cutting from a
begonia, tamping down the moss around the cutting.
Put the pot in a plastic bag, using a prop to keep the
bag from pressing on the cutting. Poke a few holes in
the bag for air circulation. The humidity in the bag will
encourage growth. Remove the bag for a few hours
each day to allow for ventilation. Once roots have
formed, transplant the cutting to potting soil.*

A luxuriant vine from an ordinary tuber

*To coax a sweet potato into sprouting, start by sticking
toothpicks around its middle (below, left). Put the
potato into a jar, narrow end down, resting the
toothpicks on the rim to keep the tuber from slipping
in. Fill the jar with water and put it in a dark place.
After about two weeks, roots and sprouts will develop.
Set the jar on a sunny windowsill and watch the vine
grow (below, right). Be sure to replenish the water.*

A mold garden grown from spores

The same mold that is unwelcome in your kitchen can teach your child that all plants do not have leaves, stems, and roots. Give him a slice of moldy bread and some fresh fruit or vegetables and have him place them in a jar. Cover the jar with plastic to seal in moisture and place it in a warm, dark location. In a few days, the mold will have spread, carpeting the food in a kind of blue-green velvet.

Simple Plant Experiments for Curious Children

You might ask your child if plants get thirsty. Give him two pots containing identical plants. Have him place the pots next to each other in a sunny window, watering the plants in one pot as needed and withholding water from the other. Inevitably the drier plants will wilt. Let him revive them with a drink.

To demonstrate how a plant absorbs moisture, fill a glass with water and add red food coloring. Cut the end off a celery stalk and place the cut end in the glass. Wait a day, then remove the stalk from the water. Slice across the stalk, exposing the dye-stained veins.

Nearly all plants are attracted to light. To show this, place several in a sunny spot on a windowsill. After a few days, point out how the leaves have angled themselves to catch the sun. Rotate the plants slightly and check daily to see whether the leaves have shifted.

Getting Down to Earth

As your child grows, so can his budding interest in plants, especially if you take the time to involve him in outdoor gardening projects. For a two-year-old, this may mean little more than being a watchful participant as he tags along in your footsteps while you sow spring flowers or set out the season's vegetables. To keep him busy, you might give him a toy shovel or watering can to play with. A three- or four-year-old, however, should be encouraged to take a more active role in the planting, helping you water newly sown seeds, weed, or any other task suited to his developing skills. A five- or six-year-old may be eager and ready enough to tend a small patch of his own under your supervision.

Such activities allow your youngster to come closer to nature and to develop a more positive attitude toward living plants. At the same time, helping you with the gardening chores—or tending his own garden—offers a valuable lesson in responsibility. And while there is always work to be done in the garden—whether turning over the soil, fertilizing it, or transplanting seedlings—each step has its own rewards, culminating in the harvest of fresh flowers or fresh fruits or vegetables.

If you live in an apartment or lack access to a plot of ground, your child does not have to miss out on the fun. The principles used in backyard gardening also apply to container gardening—in which seeds are planted in pots and grown on the balcony or in window boxes.

Whatever form it takes, outdoor gardening can build on the lessons your youngster learned indoors when he planted a sponge garden or grew his own begonia from a cutting (pages 14 and 16). He will learn more about the life cycles of plants over the course of the growing season, as he watches the seeds sprout, develop stems and leaves, then flower and produce seeds of their own. Uncovering earthworms while tilling the garden may prompt a discussion of the valuable role these lowly creatures play in aerating and fertilizing the soil. To give him a better idea of how these worms work, you might encourage him to start his own wormery (page 21). At some point, perhaps while watering or fertilizing plants, you can tell him how plants draw water and nutrients from the soil, reminding him of his experiment with the celery stalk (page 17). You might also explain how a plant's leaves need sunshine to grow and how the plants help make all life possible by breathing in "bad" air (carbon dioxide) and breathing out "good" air (oxygen).

How to Plant a Child's Garden of Delights

As every experienced gardener knows, a good garden—even a tiny one in which your child is to be a participant—begins with careful planning. Before you ever sink a spade into the dirt, you first have to decide not only how big a patch you want, but also the best place to locate your plants. For a vegetable garden, choose a sunny location where the soil is loose and crumbly and the drainage is good. Be sure to explain to your youngster your reasons for your choice. For flower beds, you can be more flexible; some flowers thrive in sunlight while others will do equally well in shade, and you will want to point this out to your little helper. Be sure, too, that you choose plants that are suited to your area's climate.

Include your youngster as much as possible in the planning. Let him thumb through a seed catalog and show you the plants he likes. Together, you can sketch your prospective garden on paper, using the catalog or gardening book to help you decide exactly what to plant and how much space to allow each planting. If you want, you can set aside one corner of the garden for an older child to try his green thumb; radishes and peas are good choices for young gardeners to plant because they grow quickly. If you prefer flowers to vegetables, you might want to plan your garden around a color scheme—mixing and matching flowers of varying hues. Or you might settle on a few special plants—four-o'clocks, whose blossoms open in the late afternoon; sunflowers, which grow over six feet tall and rotate with the sun; impatiens, which bloom profusely and produce seed pods that pop when touched.

Preparing the Soil

Even soil needs to be fed, a fact that may intrigue your young gardener. Home gardens rarely have the kind of rich, fertile loam that plants thrive in, so once you have decided where to put your garden, your next step is to test the soil for nutrient levels. An inexpensive soil-test kit that you can buy at a garden center will tell you what nutrients your soil needs.

Most gardens benefit from the addition of organic matter— peat moss, manure, or humus from a compost pile—especially if your soil is hard or sandy. Ideally, one-third to one-half of your final soil mix should consist of organic matter. In many areas of the country, you may need to work in some lime. If you live in one of the western states where the soil is more alkaline, a treatment of sulfur may be in order. Then use a spade or tiller to cultivate the soil to a depth of one foot, taking care to break up any large clods of dirt. Remove any rocks you come across, saving them, if you wish, to form a border around your garden. Here, your youngster can make a contribution of his own, piling the rocks up for you and helping with the laying of the border. Finally, rake the soil until it is smooth and level, as the grandmother and grandson on the opposite page are doing.

Planting Seeds and Seedlings

Once the soil has been dug and raked smooth, you and your assistant can begin planting either directly in the ground or by first sowing the seeds indoors in containers and later transplanting the seedlings to the garden. Most root crops and many other vegetables are suited to the first method, while more delicate plants, such as tomatoes, peppers, and many flowers, are best started indoors and moved outside after all danger of frost has passed. Starting them indoors gives your child a chance to watch their day-to-day progress.

To sow seeds in the earth, first consult your garden plan and mark the location of the first row by driving two stakes into the ground, at an appropriate distance from each other. Connect the stakes with a length of string. With the string as a guide, use the handle of a rake to make a straight, shallow furrow. Following the seed packet instructions, sow the seeds and cover them with a thin layer of soil. Warn your youngster about not packing the soil down too hard. A gentle tamping with his palm or the back of a hoe is all that is needed. Plant subsequent rows similarly.

Growing transplants indoors begins with the planting of seeds in trays or pots filled with a packaged soil mix. Cover the seeds lightly with sphagnum moss or soil mix and place the trays or pots in a sunny location. Use a plant mister to keep them damp. After the seeds have germinated and put out a pair of fully formed leaves, carefully separate the seedlings and plant them in small, individual peat planters. Be sure to water them regularly. When it is time to transplant them, move the rooted seedling, planter and all, into the prepared garden. An alternative is to buy seedlings at a nursery and transfer them to the soil, with your child digging the holes.

Watering Your Plants

Throughout the growing season, you and your youngster will need to water the garden, especially if rains are infrequent in your area. You should water—and water well—whenever the soil looks dry, saturating it to a depth of three to four inches. Early morning is the best time, since this gives the roots and surrounding soil a chance to dry out by nightfall. Show your child how to use the hose's fine spray and to administer only as much water as is required.

Nurturing the Garden

Plants need nurturing just as children do, and you can demonstrate this to your child by weeding the garden, tilling the soil, and fertilizing it from time to time. Explain that weeding keeps the soil free of wild plants that compete with your flowers or vegetables for water and nutrients. Teach your child how to pull them up, making sure that he removes the roots and not just the stems. He can help you spread a layer of mulch—an inch or two of peat moss, straw, compost, grass clippings, or other organic matter—that will control weed growth while conserving soil moisture.

Whenever you weed, take a few minutes to cultivate your garden too, using a hoe to loosen the soil around the plants so that they can absorb water more readily. To ensure that your plants have a steady supply of nutrients, fertilize the garden once or twice during the growing season. An organic fertilizer, such as manure, blood meal, compost, or fish meal, is best, although you can also choose from any number of commercial dry or liquid products.

Harvesting the Rewards

Perhaps the most exciting part of gardening for your youngster—and for you—is reaping the fruits of your joint labors. This means picking vegetables as they ripen and eating them while they are still garden fresh. Flower gardeners can take pride in seeing their hard work blossom into an array of blooms. Show your child how to take cuttings and then arrange the flowers in a vase or bowl for the family to enjoy.

Being Aware of Hazards

Gardens have their perils. Chemical insecticides, herbicides, and factory-made fertilizers pose threats to small children and animals. You may thus forgo using chemicals and rely instead on organic fertilizers and natural methods of pest control.

Use an insecticide or weed killer only when necessary and with caution—and without your child as a helper. Follow the instructions on the label carefully. Do not pour the chemical into an unlabeled container that might be mistaken for another substance later, and never apply it on a windy day. When finished, wash your hands and clothing. Safely store any leftover chemicals in their original containers. Chemical fertilizers are also dangerous, if ingested, so store them securely as well.

Plants are a leading cause of poisoning among preschoolers. There are more than 700 poisonous plants in the Northern Hemisphere alone. Most often, the culprit is poison ivy, but many others, including azaleas, poinsettias, hydrangeas, and buttercups, cause problems when ingested. Tomato leaves, holly berries, and daffodil bulbs are also poisonous, and there are more than a hundred varieties of poisonous mushrooms, some of them deadly. Even if a plant is not toxic, your child should not eat its parts; they can harm his digestive system.

If your child ingests a poisonous plant or chemical, call your regional poison-control center immediately. Do not give him anything to eat or drink until you receive medical instructions.

Earthworms at work

What has no ears and no eyes, eats dirt, and is the gardener's best friend? The earthworm, of course. With its constant tunneling it aerates the soil and fertilizes it with its droppings. To see the animal's effect, fill a large jar with alternate layers of dark, moist soil and light sand and drop in some worms. Add some dead leaves for food, punch air holes in the lid, and wrap the jar in dark paper. Every few days, add more leaves and some drops of water. After a week or so, remove the paper and have a look—the worms will have mixed the layers (below, right).

Sharing a Spectacular Transformation

Of all nature's wonders, the metamorphosis of a homely caterpillar into a winged butterfly is one of the most spectacular. And it is a wonder your child can see firsthand, with very little trouble on your part.

The process, illustrated here with a black swallowtail butterfly, consists of four stages—egg; larva, or caterpillar; pupa, or chrysalis; and adult. It begins when a female butterfly lays eggs on the plants that her species prefers as food. Soon, tiny caterpillars hatch, eat their old eggshells, and begin nibbling the nearby leaves. The caterpillars continue to feed and grow for several weeks, molting, or shedding, their skins as their growth outpaces the capacity of their skin to stretch. When the caterpillars are ready to pupate, they stop feeding and wander about in search of a place to attach themselves and develop a protective shell, or chrysalis, as the black swallowtail crawling along a garden rope is doing at right. Now is the time to capture a caterpillar to rear so your child can observe the miraculous process.

The best place to locate a specimen is on the plants that caterpillars favor. For example, you might find black swallowtails in a parsley or carrot patch, monarch caterpillars on milkweed, and clouded sulphur caterpillars on clover. Place your find in a large jar. Punch holes in the lid for ventilation. Put in a few sprigs of the caterpillar's favorite food and replenish the supply as needed. Keep the leaves moist, just as dew or rain would, by sprinkling them occasionally with water or spraying them with a mister. Stand a few twigs at an angle against the side of the container for the caterpillar to crawl up and hang from when it is ready to pupate.

After the caterpillar has formed its chrysalis, it may spend up to two weeks in this protective shell as its body undergoes enormous changes. If your child is lucky, she may see the shell split apart and the butterfly emerge. At first, its wings will be moist and weak, but soon they will expand and dry out. Caution her not to harm the fledgling by touching its delicate body. Once the wings are dry, remove the container top and let the butterfly fly free near the garden or field where you found it.

The black swallowtail butterfly begins life as a tiny, honey-colored egg that the mother lays on the stem or leaf of a parsley, parsnip, celery, or carrot plant. The egg hatches in eight to ten days, and a black-and-white caterpillar wiggles out. The tiny insect is at first camouflaged to look like a bird dropping, nature's way of preventing it from becoming another creature's meal.

For the next thirty days, the little caterpillar eats ravenously, shedding its skin repeatedly to allow for growth. When fully grown (above), it has become a two-inch-long green caterpillar with black bands, yellow spots, and two orange glands on its head for warding off enemies. By touching the glands, you can activate them and smell the unpleasant odor they emit.

The fully grown caterpillar spins a pad of silk on a twig and attaches itself head downward. After a final molt, it enters the pupal stage of development, its skin hardening into a protective shell, or chrysalis. Inside the chrysalis, the well-fed caterpillar's body turns into a creamy liquid from which the wings, legs, eyes, and feelers of a butterfly are formed.

After about two weeks, the chrysalis splits and out crawls a wet, crumpled butterfly. The delicate creature will rest for a few minutes as blood from its abdomen fills its veins, straightening its body and expanding its wings. After fanning its wings dry, the butterfly flutters off on the first flight of its month-long life span before the cycle is repeated.

Uncovering Surprises Everywhere

Wherever you live, nature is always near, with entire worlds to discover in the canopy of the trees, in the carpet of the grass, or beneath the surface of rocks. Even a city block may be home to a surprising number of living things, while a country or a suburban backyard can be a veritable wilderness, teeming with birds, insects, squirrels, chipmunks, and other wild creatures. In some areas, raccoons, rabbits, foxes, and coyotes have adjusted to living close to humans.

Anywhere your excursions take you, think of the area you are exploring as a miniature nature reserve with its own little world of plant and animal life. Encourage your child to look, to listen, to feel, and to smell. Nothing should be too trivial for observation and no aspect of nature beyond the realm of speculation.

Enough discoveries will probably come your way in the course of a neighborhood stroll that you need have no greater goal in mind than to simply enjoy each other's company as you go about making your discoveries. On the other hand, you may wish to organize your outings by setting aside a special time and assigning a theme to each nature walk, in keeping with the season. You could set out in the spring or summer, for example, with the idea of cataloging the sights, smells, and sounds unique to those months, including, perhaps, the songs of birds, the hum of bees, or the smell of freshly mowed grass. Likewise, late fall, when the leaves are off the trees, lends itself to a hunt for a bird's or squirrel's nest, while winter is the time to search for animal tracks in the wake of a fresh snowfall.

To focus your child's attention, you might want to limit your explorations to one class of living things at a time—insects one day, birds the next, flowers or trees on still another. Or you could restrict your explorations still further by looking for certain kinds of bugs, taking a morning ant or spider walk, for example, or a late-afternoon bee hunt. Along the way, you can inform your child that spiders have eight eyes yet see so poorly that they depend on their sense of touch to feel their way through their silky webs; or that young spiders searching for new homes can float through the air on strands of silk for hundreds of miles. Bees are just as fascinating. You can explain how their insatiable hunger for nectar ensures the pollination of flowers and trees, and how the buzz your youngster hears whenever a bee zips past her ear does not come from the insect's mouth or throat but is actually the sound of air being vibrated by the creature's fragile but powerful wings.

Other suggestions include having your youngster study a tree and the life it harbors, from roots to leaf tips *(right)*. You can give your youngster a magnifying glass or cardboard tube through which to peer to help him focus his investigations on a small area *(page 28)*. Or you might want to take a "blind" hike, donning blindfolds and using only your ears and sense of smell, or the sense of touch in your hands and feet, to explore the outside world. Try varying the time of day for your nature walks, venturing out in the early morning when birds and animals are more active, or on a summer evening to capture fireflies or moths.

There are so many different ways to look at the world around you, and if your backyard or local park ever does begin to look too familiar, you have only to change your perspective. You and your child can pause to explore that same world on your backs, stretching out on the grass and looking up at the trees or watching the clouds as they pass by far overhead, for example. Or you could crawl about on your hands and knees *(page 27)*.

In addition to these activities—and those on the following pages—you can help your youngster build a nature collection of rocks, feathers, or leaves *(pages 104-109)*. Together, you can turn your backyard into a miniature wildlife refuge by setting up feeders, planting nectar-producing flowers, and installing birdhouses and birdbaths.

Befriending a tree

One way to foster a better understanding of nature is to encourage your youngster to adopt a tree in his backyard or neighborhood. With your help, he can keep track of his tree throughout the seasons, using a scrapbook to note changes. The scrapbook might contain photographs of the tree at different times of year; samples of its leaves, fruits, and flowers; the child's own drawings of the tree; notes about birds, insects, and animals living in the tree; even bark rubbings. Just as people can be identified by their fingerprints, trees can be identified by their bark. To make a rubbing, tie a piece of plain paper to the trunk and then have your youngster rub a thick crayon held on its side against the paper (below). To see how well your child knows his tree, get him to explore several trees, blindfolded, using all of his senses except sight (left). Ask him to identify his own tree. Then remove the blindfold so that he can see whether he was right.

A lesson in traveling seeds

*To show how immobile plants get about, demonstrate
seed dispersal—as this mother is doing with a
dandelion. While dandelion seeds float like tiny para-
chutes on the wind, those of maple and elm trees
whirl to the ground like miniature helicopters. Other
seeds spring from a pod at the lightest touch or
have tiny barbs that hook into the hair of animals.*

A whistle from a blade of grass

Imagine your child's disbelief when you tell him you can make grass whistle—and his glee when you succeed. Simply take a single blade and place it lengthwise between your thumbs, holding tightly, as the older brother above is doing. Cup your hands, place your lips against your thumbs, and blow gently across the blade and into your palms. Now let your child try. He may be too little the first time, but soon he will be able to master this age-old childhood feat.

On hands and knees through a hidden realm

What does the world look like from flat on the ground? To find out, have your child lie on his stomach and carefully explore the ground beneath him. Ask him what grass looks like from this vantage point, whether the earth smells damp or dry, or if he can hear any insect noises. When you have exhausted the possibilities for discovery, have him crawl along on his hands and knees (left). Ask him again to describe what he sees, hears, feels, and smells.

A makeshift insect collector

An ordinary umbrella can be used to gather a shower of insects. Let your youngster hang the open umbrella upside down on the branch of a tree while you or he shakes the branch or hits it with a stick. Using a light-colored umbrella will make it easier to spot the insects. A white sheet spread on the ground also works well.

Bringing nature into sharper focus

The cardboard tube from a roll of bathroom tissue makes a splendid toy telescope that a child can use to examine small creatures, such as an insect on the bark of a tree (below). You can also tape two tubes side by side to form play binoculars and add a neck strap by slipping a string through two small holes punched in the outside edges of each tube.

A winter bug hunt

A boy inspects a neglected remnant of fall, a snowy spider web. In many parts of the country, winters are too rigorous for insects, and many species wait out the season in a state of dormancy, sometimes in egg cases, like the praying mantis, or in cocoons, like moths. Others remain partly active, if only in sheltered or sunny nooks. Finding them is not easy, but it offers a diversion for a child on a cold winter's day.

Controlling a pest

Your child should know that nature has its pests, among them gypsy moths, and that he can play a hand in controlling them. One way to vanquish leaf-stripping gypsy moth caterpillars is by hand. Between May and July, when the insects are most active, tie a string around the trunks of their favorite trees—oaks and hickories. Slip pieces of burlap under the string. Fold the burlap over the string to form an enticing spot for the caterpillars. You and your child can check the trap daily and destroy any caterpillars.

Pitfall for nocturnal insects

This simple homemade trap can give your youngster a closeup look at many shy nocturnal insects, including beetles, earwigs, centipedes, and wood lice. To lay the trap, dig a hole just large enough to accommodate a glass jar or plastic food container with the rim flush with the surface. Place a bit of cheese or meat inside as bait, then put a cover over the trap, propped up with stones on either side so that a passing bird or animal cannot steal the bait. Check the trap in the morning and examine the catch before letting the insects go.

A grab bag of nesting materials

Most children will love helping birds get ready for nesting. Over the winter, have your little one gather lengths of string, yarn, and ribbon, clothing strips, dryer lint, even the clippings from her haircuts. Then in spring, put the collection of nesting materials in a mesh bag and hang it in a tree near enough to your home so that she can watch from a window as the birds help themselves to this windfall of building supplies.

A corn feeder

Rabbits and squirrels are so fond of corn that you can use that weakness to lure the animals into your backyard. Drive a few 10- or 12-penny galvanized nails through a foot-long length of board, then push an ear of corn onto each nail. Place the feeder within sight of a window, so your child can watch the animals feed.

Concocting a bird treat

Birds, like children, love peanut butter. This little girl is spreading peanut butter mixed with melted fat between the scales of a pinecone. The fat helps the bird swallow the peanut butter without its beak sticking together. Once coated with peanut butter, the pinecone is rolled in birdseed and hung from a tree branch.

An avian Christmas tree

To turn a backyard tree into an avian restaurant, prepare a smorgasbord of bird treats to string on a length of fishing line or cord—popcorn, grapes, cranberries, seed cookies, pinecones spread with peanut butter and fat, scooped-out grapefruit halves filled with a mixture of peanut butter, fat, and seed. Then hang the treats on the tree, as the boys here are doing.

Understanding the Weather

Often unpredictable and sometimes exasperating, the weather is a universal topic of conversation. But unless your livelihood depends upon it, you may have never given much thought to how weather works. For children, the weather remains a mysterious riddle. Why is the air cold in winter and warm in summer? Where does the wind come from? What are clouds and rain and snow?

Helping your child understand such phenomena can be a source of fun—and knowledge—for both of you. A good place to begin is by encouraging him to keep a weather chart *(below)*. With it, each day's weather can become a springboard for investigating his weather riddles. Thus, a windy day is the perfect time to talk about the movement of air. Draw his attention to the wind's effect on clouds, leaves, flags, or smoke. Point out the ways in which the wind helps people—how it powers windmills and fills the sails of boats—as well as its potential to wreak destruction in the form of tornadoes and hurricanes.

Likewise, encourage your child to study the clouds. On a brisk day, they may be zooming through the sky, whereas on a foggy day, he will actually be standing in the middle of one. Clouds form, you can explain, when heat from the sun causes water to evaporate, the process by which water changes from a liquid to a vapor. The heat makes the vapor rise into regions where colder air can wring rain, sleet, hail, or snow from the clouds. To demonstrate how precipitation happens, hold a tray of ice over a kettle of boiling water. As the steam, or vapor, hits the cold tray, it condenses, or changes back to liquid, causing "raindrops" to form on the tray. Thunderstorms, too, become more fascinating than frightening when you explain that thunder is the sound lightning makes and is caused by the collision of cold air and warm air in the sky.

An older child may enjoy trying his hand at predicting the weather by learning to recognize various cloud shapes *(opposite)* and by setting up a simple weather station. All he has to do is mount a thermometer in a shady spot three to five feet above the ground, together with a homemade weather vane *(page 35)* and a rain gauge fashioned from a clear plastic cup on which you have marked off the depth in inches. You can help him keep a weather diary by jotting down in a notebook each day's date, temperature, wind direction, and overall conditions, including, after a storm, the number of inches of rain that fell.

DECEMBER

SUN	MON	TUE 1	WED 2	THUR 3	FRI 4	SAT 5
6	7	8	9	10	11	12
13	14	15	16	17	18	19
20	21	22	23	24	25	26
27	28	29	30	31		

Charting the days

This little boy is recording the day's weather by drawing a symbol on his weather chart. With adult help, he has laid out a grid of squares on a sheet of paper, labeling the squares with dates and the days of the week. He has made up his own symbols to represent different weather conditions—a sun for sunny, a cloud for cloudy, a sun and cloud for partially cloudy, vertical lines falling from a cloud for rainy, x's for snowy, and a kite pushed by horizontal lines for windy.

Reading the clouds

The various shapes that clouds assume are important indicators of future weather. By learning to recognize a few of them, your child can play weather forecaster. The wispy mare's tails, or cirrus clouds (above, left), are a sign that new weather is coming. They signal the approach of warm air and mark the boundary between it and a mass of cold air. The mackerel sky (center), made up of cirrocumulus clouds, is a harbinger of rain, while the towering thunderhead, or cumulonimbus (right), indicates a developing thunderstorm.

Where did the water go?

After a cloudburst, a boy sails a toy boat in a huge puddle (above), but a few days later finds the boat high and dry. Why? The answer lies with the water cycle, the system that conveys moisture from the earth's surface into the air and back again. Heat from the sun caused most of the water in the puddle to evaporate and rise into the air as vapor, becoming part of the clouds. When the air cools, the vapor will condense and fall back to earth again as rain, sleet, snow, or hail. The rest of the puddle soaked into the ground, where it will run off as ground water to an ocean, lake, or river or be absorbed by plant roots and eventually be transpired back into the air by leaves.

Distinguishing snow and ice

With a simple wintertime experiment, a three-year-old can discover the different forms water can assume. Show her how snow consists of delicate crystals, frozen droplets of vapor. Then have her fill a plastic cup with snow (above, left). Let her bring the snow-filled cup indoors and encourage her to wait as the warmth of the house slowly melts the snow into water, just as the sun would do outdoors. Point out how the cupful of snow (whose volume had been expanded by air) converts into a much smaller amount of water (above, right). Next, have her take the cup back outside, where instead of vaporizing and re-forming into snow, the water soon freezes into solid ice.

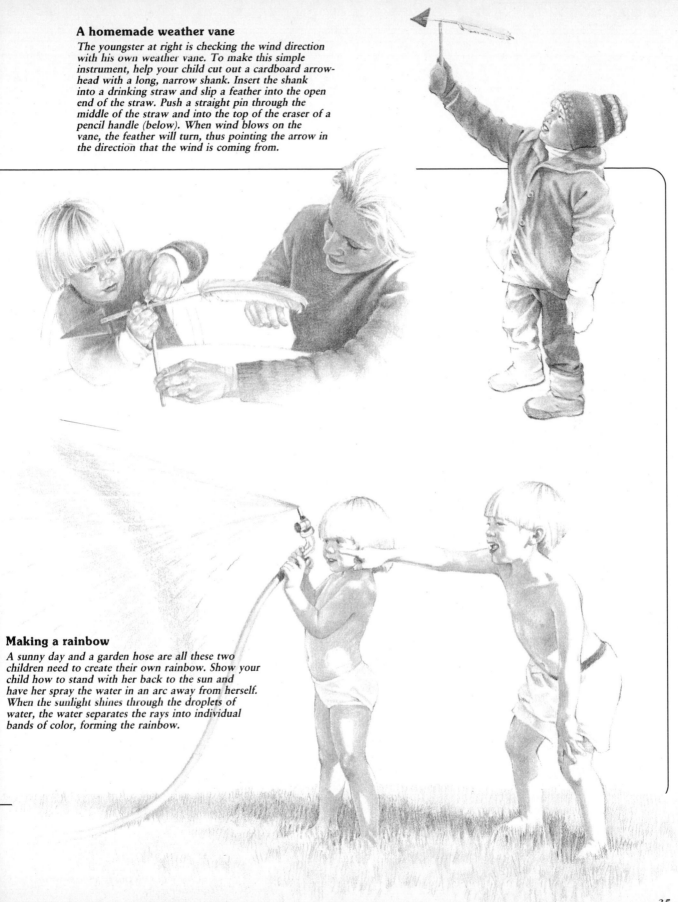

A homemade weather vane

The youngster at right is checking the wind direction with his own weather vane. To make this simple instrument, help your child cut out a cardboard arrow-head with a long, narrow shank. Insert the shank into a drinking straw and slip a feather into the open end of the straw. Push a straight pin through the middle of the straw and into the top of the eraser of a pencil handle (below). When wind blows on the vane, the feather will turn, thus pointing the arrow in the direction that the wind is coming from.

Making a rainbow

A sunny day and a garden hose are all these two children need to create their own rainbow. Show your child how to stand with her back to the sun and have her spray the water in an arc away from herself. When the sunlight shines through the droplets of water, the water separates the rays into individual bands of color, forming the rainbow.

Introducing the Wonders of the Heavens

The continually changing sky is an endless source of fascination for children of all ages. Even toddlers know the difference between day and night—if only because night means bedtime. And prompted by storybooks or television, many older preschoolers may imagine themselves soaring through the sky into space, even if they have little understanding of what space is.

The projects on the following pages—bolstered by your own simple explanations—will build on your child's growing curiosity about the heavens. The most visible of those phenomena is the sun. Your youngster may already have an idea of the sun's supreme importance in providing light and heat to the earth from the gardening and weather projects you have done together.

You will have to tailor your explanations to fit your child's age, of course, but virtually all children will be interested in finding out what makes the night dark. Night, you can explain, is darker and colder than day because one side of the earth is always facing away from the sun. A globe will help you describe how the earth rotates. Show where you live

and then shine a stationary flashlight on the globe as you spin it, demonstrating day and night.

An older child might be more curious about the relationship of the sun to the earth. Point out that the sun and the earth—and eight other planets in addition to the earth—share the same neighborhood, or solar system, in space, with the sun, a star, at the center.

Stars exert their magic pull on children's imaginations. You might tell your youngster that some are clustered in groups called constellations. With the help of a chart (*page 38*), you can locate several with the naked eye, and by shining a strong flashlight toward them, you can help your child locate them too. At these stargazing sessions, you can point out that even though he is standing perfectly still on the ground, he is actually moving, because the earth itself is hurtling through space as it travels around the sun. Nobody falls off, of course, because of gravity, the force that keeps his feet on the ground the same way it pulls back a ball tossed in the air. But because of the earth's spin, the constellations will appear to shift throughout the night.

Demonstrating the earth's rotation
With a stick and some wooden blocks, this little boy learns that the sun shines from a different angle each hour because of the earth's rotation around it. At 9:00 a.m., he set the stick in the ground and marked the end of the shadow cast by the sun with a block. He did this for each hour up to 3:00 p.m. The shadow at noontime is shortest because that is when the sun is more directly overhead.

Learning the phases of the moon

In a darkened room, with a flashlight for a sun and a tennis ball for a moon, a mother shows her daughter, who pretends to be the earth, different phases of the moon. During the moon's orbit of the globe, varying amounts of its surface are illuminated at night by the sun (diagram). The cycle begins with a new moon, when no sunlight strikes the side facing earth. The climax occurs when the moon is full and its entire face is illuminated (top). A half-moon occurs when half the face is illuminated (left).

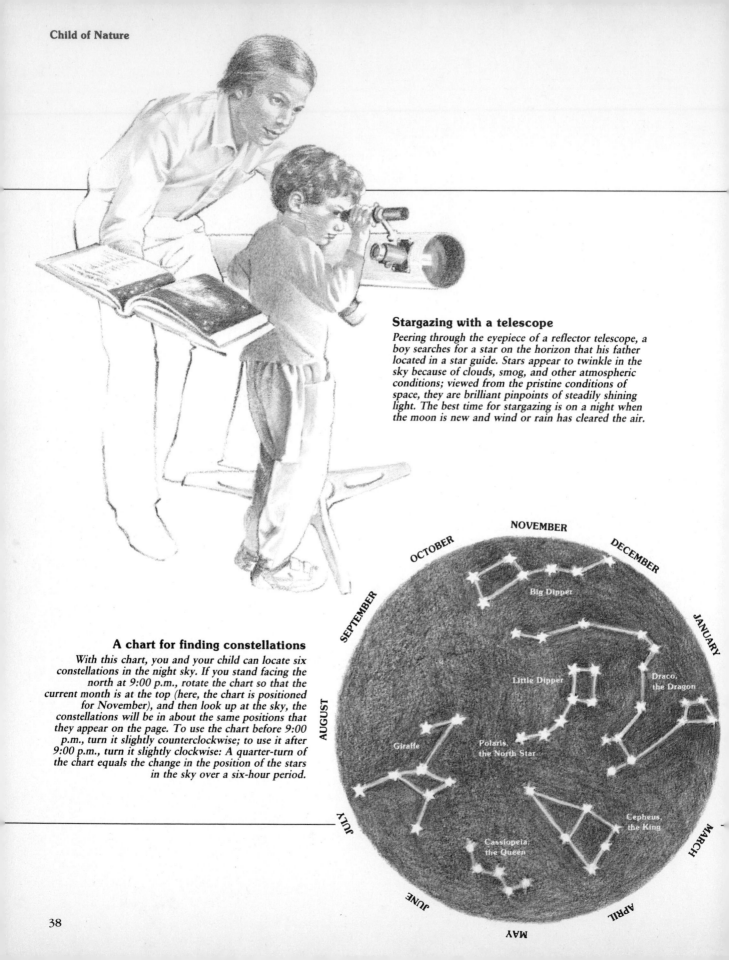

Stargazing with a telescope

Peering through the eyepiece of a reflector telescope, a boy searches for a star on the horizon that his father located in a star guide. Stars appear to twinkle in the sky because of clouds, smog, and other atmospheric conditions; viewed from the pristine conditions of space, they are brilliant pinpoints of steadily shining light. The best time for stargazing is on a night when the moon is new and wind or rain has cleared the air.

A chart for finding constellations

With this chart, you and your child can locate six constellations in the night sky. If you stand facing the north at 9:00 p.m., rotate the chart so that the current month is at the top (here, the chart is positioned for November), and then look up at the sky, the constellations will be in about the same positions that they appear on the page. To use the chart before 9:00 p.m., turn it slightly counterclockwise; to use it after 9:00 p.m., turn it slightly clockwise: A quarter-turn of the chart equals the change in the position of the stars in the sky over a six-hour period.

OCTOBER NOVEMBER DECEMBER SEPTEMBER JANUARY AUGUST JULY JUNE MAY APRIL MARCH

Big Dipper

Little Dipper

Draco, the Dragon

Giraffe

Polaris, the North Star

Cepheus, the King

Cassiopeia, the Queen

Creating a constellation box

A good way for your child to learn about constellations is to make his own representation of the most familiar one, the Little Dipper, which includes Polaris, the North Star. Have him remove both ends of a cardboard cylinder, such as an oatmeal or a salt box, cover one end with black construction paper, and using a map of the heavens as a guide, poke holes through the paper to represent the stars (above). By shining a flashlight inside the cylinder in a dark room, he can see how the constellation appears in the night sky. Then take him outside and help him locate the constellation (right).

Telling the Story of Life

Reading with his mother a book on where babies come from, a boy marvels that he started as a fertilized egg no bigger than the dot above. Such sessions help both parents and children feel at ease with the subject.

Sooner or later your child is going to begin to wonder about where she came from. Some children pursue the issue intently, some with only an occasional question. Surely how life begins is one of the most compelling stories that can be told, but it need not be told all at once. You can tell it in stages. The dilemma for many mothers and fathers is when to start. How old should a child be before a parent brings up sex? Is it even appropriate to talk to a toddler about reproduction? Or is it better to wait until a child is older?

Many experts in the field of childhood sex education think that if you wait until your youngster asks about sex, you have probably waited too long. Children do wonder how babies happen, and they are perfectly capable of learning about aspects of the process before they are old enough to formulate questions concerning it. The parent who chooses to say nothing about sex may lead her child to think that this subject is different from others and somehow taboo.

Early and reasonable sex education can have a beneficial effect on your youngster's growing self-esteem. Your positive treatment of sex helps build your child's healthy sense of self. Besides, by laying the groundwork when she is young, you will make it easier to talk about sex when she is a teenager—when communication is even more vital.

When and how to begin

Again, the experts believe it is best to introduce the subject early in your child's life. Create situations that will enable you to bring up the topic, then use them as a basis for discussion. Opportunities will present themselves too in the behavior of your pets and other animals your child observes. You can also use children's books as a starting point for conversation; there are many that deal directly with reproduction.

How to answer questions

However your child's questions about reproduction come up, you should answer them briefly but factually, using the correct terms for body parts and their functions. Resorting to euphemisms rather than real names for body parts is likely to give a child the impression that something is wrong with them. Let your youngster's questions guide you, and avoid overwhelming her with overly detailed facts. A two-year-old asking about the eggs in a nest she has found may be satisfied to learn that the mother bird simply laid them, while a five-year-old may want more details. On the other hand, your child may let loose with a whole volley of questions, and you will know you have satisfied her curiosity only when she stops asking them. Remember that one of the things you are teaching her is that she can ask you questions freely and trust your answers, not just now but later in her life as well.

Three birth stories for children

On the following pages you will find three stories, about birds, cats, and human beings, that you can read with your child. Each story has been designed as a starting point for a talk about reproduction. The notes printed in the margins are intended to help you answer some of the questions your child may have. You can read these stories to your child now, no matter what her age, and she will get something out of them. The stories are also ideal for reviewing any lessons about reproduction you may have already taught your child. ⁘

An Expert's View

Talking to Your Child about Reproduction

Since sex education is best begun early, before a child picks up wrong or distorted information about reproduction, you may find the following tips helpful.

- In discussing sexuality, it is important not just to provide facts, but to pave the way for later discussions—including talks about parental and moral values.
- While many parents fear that discussing sex will encourage children's sexual experimentation, this is simply not the case. Giving information is not the same as giving permission. Ignorance, not knowledge, causes most problems.
- Use opportunities for discussions as they occur—when your child asks a question, when a TV show deals with reproduction, or when he has seen animals mate or give birth.
- Let your child guide you as to when to discuss sex and in what detail. Tell him only as much as he wants to know when he asks.

- Clarify your child's questions before you answer. His question, "Where do babies come from?" may mean, "Do babies come from hospitals or from doctors' offices?"
- Tailor your answers for a youngster's perspective; keep explanations concrete and relate them to your child's world.
- Your child is not likely to absorb everything he hears in one sitting. Plan on repeating your explanations as he gets older, elaborating on facts you presented earlier.
- If your child's questions embarrass you, remember that to him, asking about sex is like asking about the weather. Try to treat all his questions in the same matter-of-fact way.
- And relax. You will find it easier to be honest and open if you are not all tensed up.

Ronald Moglia, Ed.D.
Director, Human Sexuality Program
New York University

Birds Have Babies, Too

Not all babies are baby people. All other animals—such as birds and cats—have babies, too. And all the babies are like their parents. Only grown-up birds make baby birds. Only grown-up cats make baby cats. And only men and women can make a baby like you.

Background for Parents

A female bird has tiny eggs in her body that must be fertilized by a male in order to produce offspring. At the start, these eggs are mostly yolk.

During mating, the male bird mounts the female and presses an opening under his tail feathers against a similar opening in her body, depositing his sperm. The sperm swim up her oviduct, a tube leading to her ovary and the eggs. Fertilization occurs when the male's sperm reach the eggs.

Each fertilized egg then moves down the oviduct, acquiring the white and a protective shell. The shell stays soft, however, until exposed to air.

Children may ask questions about any aspect of this story. Remember that a question on where the birds get the nesting materials is as important as one about the birth process.

Additional readings will bring new questions. You should expect questions about the eggs in your refrigerator. It is best to explain that these eggs, laid by chickens for our food, could not become baby chicks because they were never fertilized.

When it is time to have babies, birds make nests. These cardinals are making a nest of leaves, grass, and twigs. When the nest is made, they will use grass to make a soft bed for the eggs.

The mother cardinal lays her eggs in the new, soft nest. The eggs come from a special opening in her body, and the babies are in the eggs, which keep them safe. The mother cardinal keeps the eggs warm next to her body. Inside the eggs, the baby birds grow bigger and stronger. Then the babies use their beaks to break open the shells and come out.

The baby cardinals cannot yet care for themselves. Both the mother and father bring insects, berries, and seeds to feed the babies in the nest. And the mother cardinal keeps her young babies warm under her soft feathers. When they are bigger, the baby cardinals will fly from the nest.

A Cat Becomes a Mother

Background for Parents

Reproduction in cats occurs as it does in most mammals: A sexually mature male and female mate, and the female's eggs are fertilized by the male's sperm. Unlike humans, however, cats, and many other animals, can mate only when the female is receptive—when she is in heat. Most unneutered females are in heat at least twice a year for four to seven days.

During intercourse, the male mounts the female and inserts his penis into her vagina, the opening through which the kittens will be born. The sperm swim up the vagina, through the uterus to the oviducts, the tubes leading to the ovaries and the ova, or eggs. If conception occurs, the fertilized ova—embryos—move from oviduct to uterus, implant themselves in the uterine wall, and grow into fetuses and then into kittens. During the sixty-five-day gestation, or pregnancy, each fetus draws nourishment from the mother's body through its own placenta. After birth, the kittens must start breathing, and the mother's licking helps them do this.

Cats, like people, are mammals. Their babies grow from tiny eggs into kittens inside the mother. They grow in her uterus, a place just for kittens. As the kittens grow there, her belly gets bigger. When it is time for them to come out, the mother cat needs a warm, quiet place to give birth. This boy is helping the mother cat, putting newspaper in a box where she can have her kittens.

When the kittens are ready to be born, the mother lies down. She pushes each kitten out through a special opening called the vagina. The kittens come out wet, and the mother licks them, to dry them and help them breathe.

The mother cat stays near her babies. She keeps them warm and feeds them milk from her body. When they are hungry, the kittens nurse, sucking on the nipples on her belly, and milk comes out. The milk helps the kittens to grow bigger.

A Baby Is Born

Background for Parents

Fertilization is much the same for humans as it is for other mammals: Millions of sperm in the father's semen are ejaculated through his penis into the mother's vagina. Fertilization occurs when one of those sperm enters an ovum.

Do not forget that your child's questions will be about anything and everything. Try to answer a question on why the parents are putting a mobile in the crib in the same tone as you would answer a question on human sexual intercourse. Remember that both subjects can be equally fascinating to a youngster, and your child will be no more embarrassed asking about sex than about the mobile.

A human baby grows in her mother's uterus the same way kittens grow inside the mother cat. At first, the baby is smaller than the dot over this *i*. But then she grows into a baby. As she grows, her mother and father set up a crib, where she will sleep after she is born.

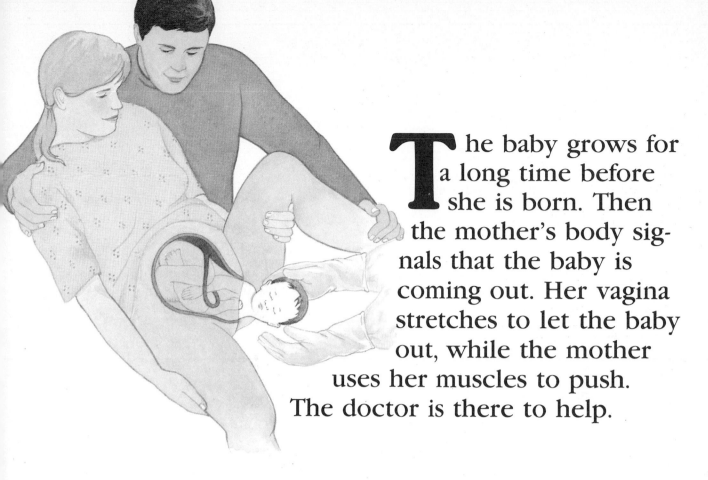

The baby grows for a long time before she is born. Then the mother's body signals that the baby is coming out. Her vagina stretches to let the baby out, while the mother uses her muscles to push. The doctor is there to help.

Once she is born, her parents take special care of her. They cuddle her, wash and dress her, and give her lots of love. They feed her when she is hungry. A baby gets milk by nursing at her mother's breast, or from a bottle.

Discovering Nature Close Up

Nature may be all around your child, offering her a chance to wonder about everything from the color of the sky to the strength of an ant able to carry a bread-crumb far bigger than itself. But there is nothing to equal the fun and excitement of a family nature outing. Fortunately, you do not have to go to the wilds to have such an outing. Almost all cities and towns provide plenty of opportunities for children to expand their appreciation and knowledge of the natural world through imaginatively contrived environments of one kind or another. You have only to think back upon your own experience as a child to remember the special thrill of visiting such places as the zoo, the natural-history museum, the local aquarium, or the arboretum. Nowadays, thanks to the advent of petting farms, nature centers, and specially designed displays, there is even more to stimulate young minds. Just imagine the thrill of the girl opposite almost rubbing noses with a dolphin. Is she likely ever to forget the moment? And won't one of the benefits of this adventure be a desire to know more about the dolphin and its wonderful intelligence?

In the pages that follow, you will find suggestions for getting the most out of the many different kinds of facilities and structured environments in your area that put nature at the disposal of your child. A measure of enthusiasm on your part, a bit of planning, and the follow-up activities you share afterward can combine to make even the simplest excursion seem more like an expedition, turning it into an enjoyable, enriching, and memorable experience for all.

Paving the Way

In planning an outing to a petting farm, zoo, or natural-history museum—or to any other environment set up to enlarge children's knowledge of the natural world—you will want to think of ways to maximize the experience for your child. Handled properly, the trip can be a perfect learning opportunity for him. Whether he is following animal tracks in the snow at a nature center or making a papier mâché giraffe at the museum, your youngster will be acquiring knowledge he can use to build a lifetime appreciation of all living things. Even a child who is only beginning to talk is not too young to respond to the excitement around him. Babies and young toddlers love imitating animal sounds at the zoo or roaming through a colorful spring garden at the arboretum. Helping your child to enjoy such visits at an early age will pave the way for longer, more focused excursions later on in his life.

Discovering where to go In your search for environments designed to bring children and nature together, you may get your best information from other parents. Ask them where they like to take their offspring for nature classes or explorations. Your child's preschool teacher also may be able to tell you about the programs at various nature sites and public institutions.

Consult your telephone book for listings under Parks and under Recreation. Or go to your nearest public library for help with finding books or magazines that detail opportunities for young children. (See page 139 for where to get the United States Nature Centers Directory, which provides information on nature centers in your area.) In many places, local newspapers run weekly schedules of family-oriented events at area museums and nature centers; and if you happen to live in a city that has a monthly magazine, you will have access to the lists of activities that it publishes as well.

Call ahead Before taking your child on an excursion, call ahead and find out about facilities. Are there toilets? Is there a restaurant or snack bar—or a picnic area where you can eat food brought from home? Can you rent a stroller, or must you bring your own? Are there accommodations for children, such as those in wheelchairs, who have special needs?

Be sure, of course, to inquire about specific programs that may be featured. Look for ones that will match your child's age, interests, and attention span. The best program will actively involve your youngster, whether in holding an animal or in assisting at a demonstration.

Reliving their recent day at the zoo, mother and daughter collaborate on a scrapbook of the girl's favorite animals. Projects like this one deepen a child's learning and serve to prolong the happy experience of a visit to a nature site.

Getting ready for the visit

In order to be sure your child will derive the most from her experience, you have to be prepared. Many centers have brochures that you can use while planning the outing. Examine these carefully; then tell your youngster where you are going and what you will see and do there. Read her some picture books about farm animals or about trees—whatever she might be expected to see on the visit. Try to find out if anything about the trip worries or concerns her, and reassure her. She may not understand, for example, that the tigers and lions she will see at the zoo will be safely behind barriers.

Take into account your child's behavior. First, take the precaution of scheduling the visit for the time of day when she is most likely to be rested and alert. Be sure she has been fed before you leave, and take along a quick and easy snack—some orange sections, perhaps, or a few crackers—in case she starts to get hungry. It may be wise to take along extra clothing as well, especially if outdoor activities are planned.

Fixing the experience in mind

After your visit, talk over what you saw together. Find out whether your youngster has questions about any of the animals or plants. See whether there were any words that he did not understand and, if so, define them for him. Stimulate his enthusiasm with questions of your own. What did he like best, and why? Which of the animals had fur, and which ones had scales? How did they move? How did the elephant use its trunk? What was special about the giraffe? Did the gorilla have a tail? Did he notice any unusual sounds or smells? The important thing is to make sure the visit really matters to your child, so that it will be a springboard for other quests to come. ❖

Down on the Farm

Young children love farms. To a child brought up in the city or the suburbs, the commonest farm animals—chickens, pigs, goats, cows, horses, rabbits—are new and exciting creatures, and even age-old chores such as milking a cow and collecting eggs have a special appeal.

Preparing your child   You will make a farm visit all the more meaningful for your child by piquing her interest beforehand. Your toddler may already have her favorite picture books and nursery rhymes about farm animals; go over them with her and tell her she will see some of the animals she likes best. Explain to her what a farm is—a piece of land used to produce food for people—and that most farms are located outside the city or suburbs. For an older child, choose storybooks about daily life on a farm, especially books that have children as central characters, and read them aloud to her before you go on the outing.

What is available   Picking a farm to visit is a fairly easy matter. You can choose between a petting farm and a living-history farm. From a child's point of view, a petting farm is fantasy fulfilled. Here the tame and obliging animals can all be touched and, depending on their size, even cuddled.

   Living-history farms demonstrate to children how farm families lived and worked in earlier times. One farm might mirror life in mid-eighteenth-century Virginia, another reflect work on a Minnesota truck farm during the 1920s. Your child may not be old enough to understand much about history, but she will learn that children in other times led lives very different from hers. She can imagine the chores they did in the house and in the fields. And all the while, she will be learning about the animals and crops the family tended.

   Many living-history farms are staffed by costumed interpreters, who go about their daily chores as though the twentieth century does not exist. Some of the hands are so steeped in history that they take on the identity of people long gone and respond in the context of the times in which the individuals they represent lived. Children find this kind of thing great fun.

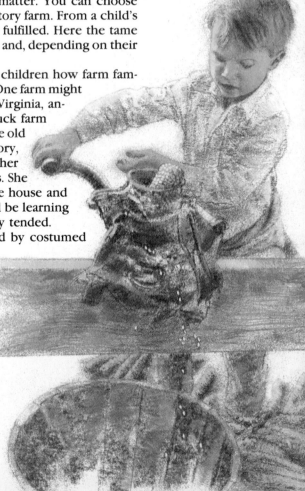

Pushing hard, a boy cranks an antique corn sheller at a living-history farm. Such experiments in food production give a child a taste of life in a bygone era, as well as a new view of the foods on his own table.

What to do when you get there

You can begin by seeking out the animals and comparing and contrasting them. Which are furry and which are feathery? How does each animal move? What does each like to eat? What kinds of sounds do they make?

A visit to a farm will provide you with a perfect opportunity to point out various connections that might otherwise elude your child. The processes of egg collecting, milking, and shearing, for example, will demonstrate to your child how important animals are for human life. Explain the link between the animals that she sees at the farm and everyday items at home—the eggs she might have eaten for breakfast, the milk that is poured on her cereal, the down stuffing in her jacket, and the wool that was used to make her sweater. Observing crops as they grow, before they are picked and shipped to the supermarket, is likely to be an eye-opening experience as well.

At many living-history farms, visitors have the opportunity to follow the steps that are required to turn plants into food for the table. Watching a gristmill at work, and then being on hand when the flour is mixed with butter and sugar and eggs to be made into cookies, or with yeast and other ingredients for bread, can leave a lasting impression on a child, one that will be pleasantly reinforced when she is invited to taste the delicious end products, fresh and warm from oven or hearth.

You might plan a special trip to a farm for a day when a large crop—such as wheat or corn—is scheduled to be harvested. Youngsters enjoy watching the harvesting machines in action, whether they are huge modern combines or more old-fashioned

A baby on a farm visit meets a goose's level gaze through the wires of the bird's pen. Even for very young children, encounters with unfamiliar animals can be fun and enlightening.

threshers and balers. You might also find it a good idea to arrange visits to the same farm several times during the growing season so your child can observe the changes that take place in the plants as they mature from seedlings to products that are ready to be harvested and brought to market.

A little something extra

Most living-history farms come with a special bonus, a chance for youngsters to witness some old-fashioned crafts and chores being executed—candle dipping, woodworking, or weaving, for example. Sometimes there is an opportunity for visitors to participate. If you sign up for one of these craft sessions with your child, be sure to choose one that she is likely to find easy and interesting. Making old-time sweets and desserts—butterscotch candies or applesauce—or decorating dried gourds for Thanks-

giving table decorations are activities that children of all ages can enjoy.

Festivals of traditional folk music are another element frequently featured by living-history farms. The concerts may be held inside one of the buildings or out-of-doors, given by one musical group or by many, in the warmth of the afternoon or the cool of the evening. Families may be encouraged to bring a picnic dinner to enjoy with the music, or perhaps to come in costume, ready to dance. Young children usually throw themselves into such events, especially if they are given the chance to sing along with the performers.

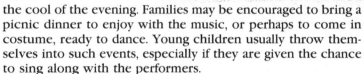

As a further enticement, many petting farms and living-history farms offer special seasonal or holiday celebrations—square dances and pumpkin-carving at harvesttime, horse-drawn sleigh rides at Christmas, hayrides in the summer. You may want to make visits to these sites part of your family's traditions.

With a quill pen homemade from a swan feather she found, a girl gets a feel for the way her ancestors wrote. To make such a pen, wash and dry the quill. With a sharp knife, cut off the tip, then slice the shaft diagonally back to front. Split the point (below). For a washable ink, add water to tempera paint.

Follow-up projects   As a way of helping to fix a farm visit firmly in her memory, suggest to your child that she draw some of the things she saw or tell you about them when you get home. Have her join you in a spirited rendition of "Old MacDonald Had a Farm," or in nursery rhymes with rural themes. Reread some of her favorite animal books and get her to point out the animals she saw at the farm and tell you how they felt to her touch. Then invite her to imitate the different sounds they made. Playact the animals together: While one of you mimics a goat, duck, or cow, the other tries to guess its identity.

Objects and products that you and your youngster bring home from the farm can be used for follow-up projects. Sheaves of golden wheat can be bent and tied into a heart shape and hung on a wall or door as decoration. Seeds and grains can be glued onto construction paper to create a textured collage, and feathers can be used to decorate a hatband. Strawberries can top off a serving of vanilla pudding or ice cream, apples can go into pie or apple butter. And if you brought a camera along, photographs in an album will be a permanent record of a special time. ∴

The Kingdom of Plants

Plants may not have quite the same fascination for children as animals do, but a botanical garden or an arboretum can still be fun for a youngster, as well as a good learning experience. He will soon discover that there is immense and fascinating variety to the plant world, from tiny prickly cacti growing in sand to giant tree ferns standing many feet tall. And in greenhouses, he will encounter a multitude of environments, from steamy rain forest to arid desert. In addition, through the special activities that are often featured at these sites, he will begin to grasp how much he relies on plants, not only for some of the foods he eats and clothes he wears, but for an essential element in the air he breathes—namely oxygen.

Two protected environments

Both botanical gardens and arboretums are designed for the culture, study, and exhibition of selected plants. They differ somewhat in the conditions—and therefore the kinds of plants—that they provide. An arboretum is an open, outdoor botanical exhibit that typically nurtures woody plants—trees and shrubs that are native to its own region or are conditioned to the climate—and thus its displays tend to be seasonal in character. A botanical garden, in contrast, encloses its exhibits within glass conservatories and can adjust conditions to mimic climates elsewhere in the world; it can therefore include many exotic plants and is able to present lush and colorful flowers and foliage all through the year.

Most botanical gardens and many arboretums offer a variety of special activities for families, including such things as building miniature terrariums, examining a seed embryo through a microscope, or making wind chimes of bamboo. Most of these centers also provide self-guided tours that parents and children can follow together. Call for details. Your local center may even offer summer-long gardening sessions in which children as young as five can plan, plant, care for, and harvest their own small vegetable gardens.

Getting ready

A child who is prepared for an outing to a botanical garden or an arboretum will be in a much better position to enjoy himself and to learn something. You can stimulate your youngster by first exploring the plant world closer to home. Depending on the time of year, carry out an indoor or outdoor planting project *(pages 14-21).* A child who has coaxed a sweet-scented bloom from a narcissus bulb in the dead of winter will be all the more eager to see a whole gardenful of blossoms in the springtime and revel in their fragrance.

On a visit to the orchid room of a botanical garden, a toddler is captivated by the bright and showy tropical flowers her mother points out to her.

To help your child understand the concept of an arboretum or a botanical garden, describe it to him as being something like a zoo where plants, rather than animals, are cared for so that people can come and look at them and scientists can study them. Show him pictures of some of the unusual plants he will see—an enormous and ancient tree, perhaps, or a very old, dwarfed bonsai, a bug-eating venus's flytrap, an orchid that looks like a butterfly. Explain that many of these plants come from faraway places where the land and climate are very different from your own. Tell him that even deserts, where soil is dry and days are hot, have many plants that grow best there. He will be fascinated to learn that desert plants have thick-skinned leaves to conserve moisture and thorns to keep hungry animals away.

You can turn a walk through a botanical garden or an arboretum into a treasure hunt—and help your child sharpen his observation skills—by asking him to search for specific shapes in the plants. Have him look first for heart-shaped leaves or flowers; then switch to a search for oval shapes or umbrella shapes. Or suggest that he try counting how many different types of flowers he can find that are of the same color. You may wish to bring a magnifying glass with you so your child will be able to examine flowers and leaves in detail. Ask him to describe what he sees: the branching veins of a leaf, the fingerlike stamens of a flower, or the pointed thorns of a cactus. Can he find any seeds? What do they look like?

Encourage your child to continue his interest in plants after he returns from the arboretum or botanical garden. You might, for example, go on a hunt in your own garden or in a local park for species that are the same as or similar to the ones he saw on the visit. You can have him start a seed collection based on the fruits and vegetables you use in your cooking. Or, drawing on your supply of lentils and dried beans and peas, you can show him their variety and then have him layer them in a jar for kitchen display. And as a final fillip, you might encourage him to select a couple of each of these and place them on wet cotton to germinate so that he can discover what baby plants look like. ❖

Outdoor Nature Centers

Located on undeveloped land, usually within a city or suburb, a nature center is a place where you and your child can see the landscape and wildlife of your local area—whether prairie, forest, or desert—as it was before urbanization. A nature center may be quite small, comprising only a few acres of untouched marshland or a mile or two of pristine shoreline; but some centers are large indeed, encompassing hundreds of acres of land and several kinds of terrain.

Unlike a botanical garden or zoo, a nature center usually contains only native plants and animals and displays them mostly in their natural habitat. In contrast to an arboretum, where native plants are actively cultivated and landscapes are often planned and constructed, a nature center is meant to preserve the land in its wild state; its caretakers alter the area only enough to make it safe and accessible for visitors. Rugged though the environment can be, nature centers generally have recreational facilities such as playgrounds, and amenities, including rest rooms, picnic tables, and a visitors' center where you can get trail maps and information about activities. Some larger centers also have small indoor exhibits, like those found in natural-history museums, where preserved specimens of lizards, frogs, insects, and other wildlife can be viewed up close. A nature center may even have a few tamed wild animals, such as rabbits or snakes, for young children to touch and hold.

A host of things to do To meet their goal of encouraging the study and appreciation of local wildlife, most nature centers sponsor a wide variety of educational and recreational activities, many of them geared to young children and their families. On daytime "critter walks," three- and four-year-olds search for signs of animals along a forest trail; during "nature at night" expeditions, five- and six-year-olds look and listen through the twilight for owls, bats, raccoons, and other nocturnal creatures. The children are guided by trained naturalists.

Many nature-center programs focus on a single animal or plant—on the beaver and its dams, perhaps, or the life cycle of a fern or water lily. Your child may already be fascinated with one such subject, and eager to learn more. Other study programs will reveal to her a world whose existence she had not suspected—the underground realm of an ant colony, for example, or the insect life under the bark of a dead tree.

A hidden benefit Through nature-center activities, your child may also learn to overcome her groundless fears about a particular kind of crea-

ture, such as a spider or a snake. Not only will she gain new knowledge of the animal—where it lives, what it eats, how it moves—but at the exhibit center she will also see adults and other children touch and examine it without fear. This experience should help dispel any negative feelings she may have about the animal—and make her less timid when encountering unfamiliar wildlife on future explorations. The guide will of course warn all visitors about any indigenous creatures that really are dangerous.

Indoor activities   Although most nature-center activities take place outdoors, many nature-related crafts and projects for children are conducted in classrooms and workshops. Youngsters may be taught how to turn discarded milk cartons into birdhouses or fashion holiday ornaments from natural materials. These indoor activities are usually combined with outside exploration. A trek through the woods in search of a wild mushroom's natural habitat, for example, may begin with a classroom dissection of that fungus's stem, cap, and gills. A butterfly-catching expedition may begin with a slide presentation showing the insect's life cycle, move on to the actual netting phase, and end indoors once again with the children drawing pictures of the butterflies they captured. Many centers have a special "nature hour" for toddlers

and preschool-
ers, in which nature songs and sto-
ries are followed by a hike along a forest trail. A reservation and
a small fee are usually required for such programs; always call
ahead to get information and to find out what provisions will be
made if the weather is poor.

Happy trails To enjoy the beauty of a nature center, you do not need an
organized activity. Nature centers have specially marked self-
guided trails *(above)* where you and your child may wander at
your ease. Simply ask for a trail guide at the visitor center, and
strike out on your own. Where you see a numbered marker
along the trail, stop and read from the guide. It may point out

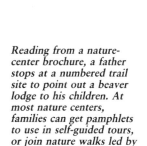

an owl's home in a hollow tree, a poison ivy vine climbing a tree trunk in search of sunlight, or a stand of mountain laurel where animals and birds shelter from the snow.

Most nature centers also have miles of unmarked trails, which you and your child may wish to roam together. Be sure, however, not to overtax his energies; his little legs may not be able to take him any great distance *(page 118)*. Some centers have bicycle paths for families who wish to explore larger areas of a particular terrain with their children. You will need to bring your own bicycle and a way of carrying your child—either in a child's seat mounted on the bike or in a wheeled cart pulled along behind. If your five- or six-year-old is a strong and safe bicyclist, he may wish to ride next to you on his own bicycle. No matter what his age or how he travels, he should always wear a helmet when he is on a bicycle.

Among a nature center's many wonderful features, not least is the opportunity it gives you to expose your child to the changing seasons. By returning to the same place at different

Reading from a nature-center brochure, a father stops at a numbered trail site to point out a beaver lodge to his children. At most nature centers, families can get pamphlets to use in self-guided tours, or join nature walks led by a staff naturalist.

Questions from Inquiring Minds

Nature inspires children to ask many questions. Answering them well takes skill. Below are some commonly asked questions—and the kinds of replies that make sense to young naturalists. You may wish to model your own answers on these.

Q. How can a fly walk on the ceiling?
A. A fly makes a glue that comes out of its feet and holds it firmly to the ceiling.
Q. Where are the snake's ears?
A. A snake has no ears; along its body, it feels vibrations—tiny movements—of such sounds as your approaching footsteps.
Q. Why does the turtle go into its shell—what's it doing in there?
A. A turtle withdraws into its hard shell for protection from enemies; it is waiting for danger to pass.
Q. Why doesn't the turtle walk all the way out of its shell?
A. A turtle's shell is part of its body; its skin and its backbone are attached to the inside of it.
Q. Why can't fish come out of the water and live in the air?
A. Just as humans get oxygen from air, through our lungs, fish get it from water, through their gills. A fish trying to breathe air will die.
Q. How can owls hunt at night?
A. The owl's large eyes are made for dim light, and its hearing is so keen that it can hear a mouse stepping on a leaf.
Q. Where does a firefly's light come from?
A. Part of the firefly's body is specially designed to make light.
Q. How can some birds sleep on trees without falling off?
A. Birds' toes have special muscles that lock in place when the birds settle down on a tree branch.
Q. Which bird is the biggest? Which is the smallest?
A. The ostrich is the largest bird in the world, and the hummingbird is the smallest.
Q. Will a worm die if I cut it?
A. If you cut off the tail or even the tip of its head, a worm can grow those parts back, but if you cut it in half it will die.
Q. Why do skunks spray that terrible smelling stuff?
A. The skunk sprays to temporarily blind its enemies, so it can escape from them.
Q. How do fish stay warm when a pond gets icy?
A. In the wintertime, the fish go to the bottom of the pond, where it stays warmer. Besides, they do not have to keep as warm as you do in order to keep alive.

times during the year, you help him learn about their cycle and the effect they have on plants and animals.

You can also help him to understand that nature stays active throughout the year, as various animals' tracks in a snow-covered meadow or marsh will readily make evident. In the springtime, when the birds are nesting, you and your child can find out how and where they nest; then, later in the season, you can go on a hike to see them with their young. In the summer-time, you can stalk katydids and learn to lure them from the treetops by imitating their sound or by playing a taped recording you previously made of their song; you can search along a muddy trail for paw prints and make plaster casts of them to take home with you *(page 96)*. In the autumn, you can walk together along a woodland trail in search of mushrooms and other fungi or learn to identify different kinds of trees by their autumn colors. And during the winter, you can spend some time trekking through the snow in warm, wetproof boots or on snowshoes, looking for signs of animals.

As with any other outdoor activity described in this book, it is helpful to ready your young-ster for the experience in advance. Browse together through field guides that show pic-tures of indigenous plants and animals. Have your little one select two or three that he wants to be sure to see during your hike and then search for them. Explain to your child that a nature center is there to preserve a part

Children visiting a nature center get a closeup view of a black rat snake in the hands of a naturalist. Many nature centers exhibit small indigenous animals, such as snakes, frogs, and mice, in cages, and most offer classes to introduce children to the area's wildlife.

of your area as it was before your town or city was built, that the land there is very much the way it was in the days of the early settlers. Having caught his imagination, tell him that the nature center is a haven for your area's plants and animals, that these living things have a hard time surviving in a built-up environment, and that visitors must not harm them. In this way, you help your child begin to see the importance of preserving wilderness—a nature center's primary objective.

A five-year-old explores the contents of a "feelie box," made by her mother from an old sock and a large juice can. Each time the mother loads the box, the two friends take turns guessing the identity of such items as shells, acorns, leaves, and pine cones that have been put inside.

What to wear Be sure everyone in your party is dressed appropriately for the visit. A change in the weather can turn what was intended as a happy experience into an unhappy one, especially if your child becomes wet or cold. Take along too much clothing rather than too little; you can always remove a sweater or extra socks if need be. In addition, be sure everyone in your party is wearing good, sturdy walking shoes or boots, with room to wiggle the toes. If you are intending to devote the greater part of the day to exploration of the nature center, hike with a small daypack for those extra articles of clothing, a simple snack, a small container of drinking water, and any field guides you deem necessary. You may also wish to take a pair of binoculars or a magnifying glass to aid your observations.

Follow-up activities To enhance your child's interest in local wildlife, follow up your visit with related projects. Take her to the public library for books about the plants and animals she saw. Find books that illustrate the life cycles of various animals, especially ones that change dramatically, such as frogs and butterflies. Encourage her to write and illustrate a story about these creatures; or help her stage a little play, enacting a caterpillar's metamorphosis into a butterfly *(pages 22-23)* or a tadpole's growth from polywog to frog *(page 91)*. ❖

Nature on Exhibit

After exposing your child to nature outdoors, you may want to take him to a natural-history museum for a wider view of the world. Through rich and varied exhibits, including such things as reconstructed dinosaurs, fossilized wood, and even moon rocks, a natural-history museum allows a youngster to explore nature across time as well as over distance. He can see things that come not only from far away and from very different parts of the world and universe, but also from other periods of the earth's history. He will glimpse the surprising world of mil-

A Tyrannosaurus rex model looms in lifelike splendor over small visitors at a children's museum. Most young children find dinosaurs irresistible and love to see these ancient behemoths on display.

lions of years ago—home to giant birds, strange plants, miniature horses, but no people. He will learn of some of the forces that have shaped the planet, from a volcano's fiery outbursts to a glacier's slow grinding action. And he will witness the immense diversity in nature today, from fish that can almost fly to rocks that glow in the dark.

What to expect A natural-history museum collects, preserves, studies, and displays specimens from the natural world, whether they be fossils millions of years old or insects recently captured in the wild and carefully mounted for study.

Adding an element of realism in every natural-history museum is the three-dimensional diorama, a scale-model or full-size replica of a natural scene, showing a specific animal in its habitat. A child may see a family of wolves in their forest den or a giant brontosaurus poised to nibble the leaves and twigs of a tall tree. You may need to reassure a particularly impressionable youngster that the animals in these lifelike displays are in fact not alive and cannot harm him.

A natural-history museum also features exhibits about human beings, showing how people in various cultures have used natural materials and affected the world around them. Displays may include ancient items—tools from the Stone Age, for example, or Roman pottery 2,000 years old—and more modern objects, such as twentieth-century weavings from Central America. Some museums even contain full-size replicas of dwellings— perhaps an African grass house or the log cabin or sod house of an American pioneer family.

As you would do with a visit to an outdoor nature site, prepare your child for the visit by explaining to her beforehand what a natural-history museum is and what she will find there. Call ahead for information, so that you will be able to name some of the exhibits that will interest her particularly. Most youngsters love dinosaurs, as well as any objects that carry superlatives before their names—the biggest diamond, the oldest tree trunk. Ask your librarian to help you find a few books that are related to the things your child especially wants to see. If you plan to spend some time with the anthropology exhibits, for instance, read stories about children from other times and other cultures.

To make a child's visit more fun—and more educational— many natural-history museums have special "touching tables" or "discovery rooms," where children can hold and examine exhibits. Here your child may feel a fossil footprint, stroke polar-bear fur, handle animal skulls, or sort through a collection of

A little girl displays a homemade diorama, inspired by those she saw on a museum visit. With her mother's help, she has used a cardboard box lid, cotton for clouds, clay for the ground, and foil for water. Bird and animal cutouts complete the scene.

ocean shells. He may shake a small can with seeds inside and then match the sound he hears to the feel of other seeds arranged for him to touch. A discovery room may also include "stumper" specimens—objects that are presented without names but with clues to their identity in the form of questions. The answers might be offered at another location in the discovery room, or they may be found in other exhibits in the museum, where the children are expected to find them.

In addition to a discovery room, your museum may have exhibits big enough to walk through or climb on—the replicated chamber of a limestone cave in which early humans lived, perhaps, or a re-created hillside with the fossils of prehistoric sea creatures embedded in it. To rouse young visitors' interest still further, many natural-history museums are peppered with pocket theaters that feature short films about certain of the nearby exhibits. Viewed at the beginning of a visit, these movies help to focus a child's attention.

Taking it in stride So that your youngster will get as much as possible out of his visit to the museum and will want to come back, plan a short visit the first time, concentrating on just one or two exhibits. When you set a relaxed pace, you keep him from feeling overwhelmed by the wealth of new information.

Let your child's curiosity tell you how long to spend with each exhibit. He will most likely be full of questions for you, but you can stimulate his thinking further—and perhaps direct it more—with questions of your own. In a cave exhibit you could ask him, "What kinds of animals do you think live in such a cave?" or

"How could you see if you were inside a cave?" or "What would it feel like to live in one?"

Home again Before you head for home, be sure to drop by the museum's shop to see whether there are any books or items to buy that might enrich your young one's learning experience. Then, after your visit is complete, talk over with her the things she saw. At the library, let her choose books about subjects she enjoyed at the museum. Read these together, and have her compare what she sees in the books with what she observed at the museum. As another stimulus, the two of you can make a project of transforming a large box into a make-believe cave for her favorite stuffed animal, decorating the cave walls with drawings of ancient animals. Or you can make a diorama in a smaller box *(opposite),* using pictures cut from magazines.

You may want to build on your child's budding interest in paleontology and archaeology by creating a small excavation site for her at home. Bury a few objects—a coin, a chicken bone, a shell, a rock on which you have drawn a fossil—in a sandbox or large tub of dirt. Give your youngster a spoon and a kitchen sieve and have her carefully dig and sift for artifacts. For a five-or six-year-old, you can make the activity even more realistic by marking off the digging area into four quadrants, with sticks and strings, just as an archaeologist would do. Then, for a simple map of the site, use a pencil to draw four quadrants on a piece of paper. As your child unearths each of the objects, have her note it with an *X* in the correct quadrant. Such an activity will help give her an understanding of the amount of care and precision scientists must bring to their digs. ⁘

Two budding entomologists examine beetle specimens in their natural-history museum's discovery room. In this room, hands-on exhibits let children explore more thoroughly some of the items shown elsewhere in the museum.

Excitement at the Zoo

A zoo is a child's paradise, a place where she can laugh at the antics of a chimpanzee, shiver at the open jaws of a crocodile, or gaze in awe at an elephant lumbering across a simulated African savanna. Besides being just plain fun, such experiences can spark in your child a greater curiosity and enthusiasm for nature. She will learn about the characteristics and habits of wild animals and how they have adapted to their environments. She will also begin to understand the importance of wildlife conservation and how the work of zoos is essential in protecting many animals from extinction.

So it will be a good visit Before you go, describe a zoo—or zoological garden—as a place where people can see wild animals from all over the world, and where scientists can study the animals. Explain also that various related animals—the bears, the wild cats, the birds, or the reptiles—are usually grouped together at a zoo. Discuss with him which kinds of animals he would most like to see, then try to limit your visit to just them, so as not to overwhelm him.

Be sure to mention a few of the more exciting animals that he will be able to see at the zoo—tigers, rattlesnakes, gorillas, and giant tortoises. Read him children's books about zoos as well as those about wild animals in their natural habitats. If your child is still a toddler, you may want to explain the difference between domesticated and wild animals. An older child will be interested in learning that zoos house and preserve many animals that are close to extinction. For example, Przewalski's horse—the world's only true wild horse—no longer exists in the wild in its native Mongolia and is found now exclusively in zoos and nature preserves.

Seeking out the animals Depending on its size, as well as on the type of animals it has, a zoo may keep its creatures in relatively small, caged enclosures or in large, open expanses that re-create their natural habitats. Some zoos specialize in showing animals indigenous to the local area; others take a more traditional approach and display animals from distant regions—Bengal tigers from India, for example, or dromedary camels from North Africa or Asia. At some zoos, many of the birds are housed in an aviary big enough for visitors to walk through. Most children love the torrent of sound that washes through these huge birdcages.

Call in advance to see whether there is a children's zoo within the zoo, where youngsters can see unusual animals up close and perhaps touch them. There may even be a camel for preschoolers to ride. If there is an animal nursery, your child may see an

Wearing protective mitts on their hands, a girl and her brother at their city's zoo enjoy a rare chance to touch an echidna—a spiny anteater—far from its native Australian habitat.

incubator where birds' eggs are hatched, or perhaps watch young monkeys being bottle-fed, just as human babies are. You will want to explain that these kinds of care are needed only when an animal's own mother cannot tend it or the baby is sick.

You both might enjoy a ride on a monorail or a double-decker bus as you take a guided tour of the zoo's outdoor exhibits. It is also fun, of course, to explore the zoo's grounds on foot. The information desk should be able to provide you with a trail map that you can use to find the areas of the zoo where your youngster's favorite animals are housed. As you plan your walking safari, however, make sure that the distances to be covered are reasonable for short legs.

Please touch   Many modern zoos have hands-on exhibits of animal-related objects, such as a rattlesnake's rattle or a raccoon's skull, for inquisitive youngsters to examine. There may even be a learning laboratory, where special activity boxes hold the directions and materials for projects that teach young naturalists about animal anatomy or behavior. Your child may be challenged to assemble the skeleton of a turtle from the bones and shell. Or he may be called upon to match feathers from a collection with those pictured in photographs of various birds. He may even get a chance to handle live animals, including such placid creatures as the box turtle and the leopard gecko lizard. These animals are chosen not only because they appeal to children, but because they are able to withstand the stress of being held and investigated by little hands.

Zoos also offer a variety of classes for toddlers and preschoolers, in which your child may learn how bats find their food in the dark, or why some animals eat meat and others plants. Call for class times, dates, and costs.

Many zoos feature daily animal demonstrations that are both entertaining and enlightening. You and your child may have the opportunity to watch seals dive for the fish their keeper throws, or leopards leap at the command of their trainers, or elephants lift huge logs with their trunks. Such demonstrations are usually presented free of charge; when you arrive at the zoo, simply ask where and when the animal shows are going to be.

Making connections

While you are making your way around the zoo during your visit, encourage your child to look for differences and similarities among the animals. Which ones are alike, and in what ways? You may want to focus on animal coverings, noting which of the animals have fur, feathers, scales, or

Three excited children sway in the saddle atop an Asian elephant during their visit to a zoo. The animal's trainer, while guiding her around her pen, gives the children a lesson in elephant care and feeding.

skin. Explain that all mammals have hair or fur on their bodies—even the seemingly hairless elephant and rhinoceros. Tell your child how a bird's feathers not only keep it warm, but also allow it to stay dry during rainstorms. Describe how the hard, dry scales on snakes and other reptiles help protect their bodies from injury and keep them from losing essential moisture from their bodies when they are in the sun. And explain to your little one that amphibians, animals that live both in water and on land, have wet, bare skins, with no scales, fur, or feathers. You may also find your zoo visit a good opportunity to introduce the concept of camouflage and how an animal's coloring provides protection from its predators or, as in the case of the tiger, allows it to sneak up on its prey without being noticed.

You may want to focus on the different ways in which animals move. Which animals walk and run? Which crawl? Which swim? Some, of course, move in several ways; a duck can swim, walk, and fly, and an alligator can swim and run.

Help your child to take notice of the differences and similarities between some of the animals in the zoo and himself. How is his neck different from a giraffe's neck, for example, or his foot different from the foot of a penguin? Which animal does he think he resembles most closely? In what ways? Explain to your child that you and he are animals, too, sharing a good many traits with other animals, especially the great apes and in particular the chimpanzees.

On familiar ground After the excitement of a zoo visit, children often want more of the experience. You might get an older child to paint a picture of her own zoo, filled with her favorite animals. To give her further insight into the way animals are classified, cut out magazine photographs or illustrations of various animals, then encourage her to sort the pictures in different ways—by size, number of legs, or outer coverings. Afterward, she can assemble the pictures into a colorful zoo collage.

Your child can also sculpt a zoo, using store-bought modeling clay or homemade modeling dough. To make the dough, combine two cups of flour, one cup of salt, two tablespoons of cream of tartar, one tablespoon of vegetable oil, and two cups of water in a large saucepan. Cook the mixture over medium heat, stirring it, until it thickens and begins to pull away from the pan. Allow the dough to cool, covered by a damp cloth so that it will not lose moisture, then remove it from the pan and knead it for a minute or so. It will then be ready for your child to mold into the creatures of her choice. ❖

Creatures of the Deep

Whether watching a sand tiger shark through the glass wall of a tank or tossing a fish to a hungry captive sea lion, a child at an aquarium or a marine park will be adding exciting new dimensions to her knowledge of nature. Here, within a relatively small area, she can learn about the watery habits and habitats of a widely diverse group of creatures—from the giant blue whale, the largest mammal that has ever lived, to the Thumbelina of frogs, the rare poison-arrow frog of South America.

Types of exhibits

Aquariums and marine parks have the advantage of being able to feature uncommon animals rarely seen outside photographs, and because these animals tend to be so different from the creatures in zoos and wildlife centers, they appeal greatly to children and adults alike. Most of the aquatic animals are displayed in large tanks simulating natural environments; your child will enjoy gazing through the glass walls and marveling at the activity within. Some of the residents that most appeal to children are the alligators, giant sea turtles, piranha, octopuses, and sea horses. Penguins are also frequently featured, as are puffins, the chunky little "sea parrots of the North Atlantic," or other exotic birds.

In addition, most aquariums and marine parks provide a range of educational activities for children. Your toddler may hear a recording of whales communicating with one another or discover what it feels like to touch a shark egg. The facility you visit may also have an "aquatheater," where she can watch trained dolphins, whales, or sea lions dive through hoops or leap to great heights. Especially geared for children are "touch tanks," housing such curiosities as starfish, sea urchins, sea horses, and horseshoe crabs. Children are encouraged to reach in and handle these creatures—without removing them, of course.

Tips for teaching your child

If your toddler has an aquarium at home, he will already be familiar with the habits and requirements of fish. If not, you may need to tell him that fish can survive only in water. Explain that they must have water for the same reason people must have air—to breathe—and that they take oxygen from the water through special organs called gills. Point out, too, that there are some animals, such as whales, that live in water but still have lungs and breathe air by coming to the surface from time to time. Be sure to mention a few of the more exciting animals he will see during his visit to the aquarium, and to engage his interest still further, read stories to him about the sea and the different animals that live in it.

At the exhibits   When you arrive at the aquarium, play a detective game with your youngster by having her look for the flattened fish that hide from their enemies by turning sideways so they will not be seen, or the bullet-shaped fish that are built for speed. Can she tell, by the sizes of their mouths, which fish eat large prey and which eat tiny plants? You might search for fish with familiar common names—squirrelfish, parrotfish, lionfish—and discuss how each got its name. Ask her to make up names for other fish she sees, based on their looks. Discuss with her how the various animals in the exhibits protect themselves from predators. Which ones use camouflage? Which burrow into the sea floor? Which carry their own protective shells?

When you get home   After an afternoon among strange and often beautiful underwater creatures, your child may want a few fish of her own as pets. Select such easy-to-care-for kinds as goldfish or guppies at a pet store, then help her prepare a small aquarium for them.

Your youngster may also enjoy making a fish mobile for her room. Cut the shapes of some of her favorite fish from heavy construction paper or thin cardboard, and have her color in their markings on both sides of the cutouts. Tie the decorated fish, using string or thread, to a slender stick or branch, and hang the mobile from the ceiling of her room. ⁘

As a friend watches, a boy gently cradles a nonstinging sea urchin in an aquarium's touch tank. The shallow tank, at waist level, lets a child meet aquatic animals in their own element.

Hailing the Seasons

You can link your child to nature in many wonderful ways. One little girl's parents marked her spring birth by planting a sapling. Every spring since then, they have taken a photograph of their daughter next to the tree. The tree is almost exactly her age, and she loves to look back at the pictures and see how they both have grown and changed.

The joy in seasons

You can enrich your family's own nature lore by participating in community-wide nature celebrations. The maple-syrup season throughout the Northeast inspires numerous events. Washington, D.C., draws thousands to its Cherry Blossom Festival each year. Punxsutawney, Pennsylvania, puts its whimsical all into Groundhog Day, on February 2. Arbor Day is observed nationwide with tree plantings, on dates suited to each state's climate. Wildlife migrations call forth many regional salutes, such as the Waterfowl Festival every fall in Easton, Maryland, and the Monarch Butterfly Celebration in Pacific Grove, California, each October, when thousands of monarchs arrive to mate. The clockwork return in spring of the swallows to Capistrano, California, has long been noted nationwide and remains an occasion for joy in the local area. Consult nature centers, conservation groups, state tourism offices, and your library for dates.

Around the year in rituals

Observing the seasons in private celebrations is still another way to instill a love of nature in your child. Autumn is for harvest rituals, and many families take advantage of harvesttime to collect fruit and make jams and jellies, or spend a day at an orchard picking apples for pies and apple butter. Halloween brings the time-honored pumpkin, and children love to help choose it, scrape out the seeds, and design the scary jack-o'-lantern face. If you roast the seeds or make pumpkin pie, your youngster learns a great lesson—the many and varied rewards of the harvest. If she plants the seeds in a pot, she can see the cycle of growth and harvest starting all over again.

The first snowfall brings not just great glee but the means for performing a ritual that has long been a favorite of New Englanders: making maple candy. Heat maple syrup until it thickens, then trickle it over fresh snow, in a bowl or out-of-doors; it will congeal into a chewy, delicious substance.

Winter is a rich time for looking inward (and indoors), especially on the winter solstice, December 21, the shortest day of the year. Many families burn candles or turn on their Christmas lights then for the first time, heralding the lengthening days that follow. For a memorable outdoor family event, visit a

December brings many families a chance to welcome winter with an outing to a Christmas-tree farm. A parent must wield the ax, but everyone can help choose and carry the family's tree.

Christmas-tree farm *(below)* and have your child help in choosing the tree. You can also have her help keep the tree stand filled with water; explain to her that the tree still requires care even after it has been cut down.

Children need scant urging to celebrate the rebirth of nature in the spring. Plan a wildflower walk through the woods, or have a first-robin party. Later in the spring, on an evening ramble at a marsh or pond, you and your child can enjoy the mating calls of thousands of frogs and toads. Point out the tiny peeper's high-pitched whistle and the bullfrog's deep croak.

In early summer, spotting tadpoles in a pond or creek will fascinate your child. Midsummer lends itself to evening rituals, such as a moonlit walk through the woods, with a flashlight, to see the fireflies and hear the full orchestra of insects—especially cicadas and crickets. With you near, your child will feel safe to enjoy the magic of the outdoor night. ❖

Where the Wild Things Are

Discovering how all the pieces of nature's great jigsaw puzzle interlock is a jubilant experience for a child. And nothing promotes this education better than a visit to an environment largely untouched by human beings. With each exposure to a new wilderness setting— forest, meadow, pond, stream, river, wetland, and desert—more and more pieces will fall into place for your youngster. Children love being detectives; tracking clues to wildlife survival will engage your young one's powers of observation and her spirit of fun. Just look at the absorption of the two young explorers in the photograph as they examine a harvest of water creatures scooped from a pond, and you will know what such an experience can mean to your child.

But for all its beauty, nature is dominated by reality, and your child's sleuthing might lead her to a few surprises. On a summer day in a meadow, chasing butterflies among the blooms, she may be upset to discover that these small, delicate creatures are eaten by birds. It is your job to assure her that this is all very normal, that birds, just like humans, must eat to live.

Although visits to natural habitats can awaken your child's curiosity, the sharpening of her appreciation depends on studying some of the plants and animals she sees. The following section illustrates activities that you can use to increase her knowledge, foster her sensitivity, and encourage her understanding of conservation. Since many children enjoy showing off their finds, the section concludes with an essay on preserving and displaying nature collections.

Developing a Respect for Wilderness

Wilderness can be a great teacher. As a parent, you have only to use your youngster's desire to touch, smell, and look closely at almost everything he encounters in your wanderings together in order to cultivate the sensitivity that will grow into an enduring respect for the wilderness and the creatures that depend upon it for survival.

Planning an expedition

Before venturing out with your child into the wilderness, spend some time talking about the natural environment you will be visiting together. Explain that just as he has a home, many plants and animals make the outdoor world their home. You might also read him a story or show him some pictures that will get him thinking about the plants and animals he may spot. Tell him that they are particularly suited to live in the wild and then help him to find what makes each one so special. As an additional stimulus, encourage him to imagine what it feels like to be a squirrel or how a nectar-seeking bee might see a flower as it comes in for a landing on the petals.

Even for an expedition only a few hours long, it pays to be prepared. Just in case your youngster becomes hungry or thirsty, carry a snack and something to drink. And to increase the meaningfulness of the outing, consider packing nature guides to identify the species you see, as well as binoculars. It pays also to pack a first-aid kit, on the off chance an injury should occur.

Ever-changing nature

Nature casts many spells, and never more of them, it can seem, than when the setting is wild. By returning to the same place at different times of year, your child can witness firsthand the effect of the seasons on the plants and animals dwelling there. By observing sites at dawn and at dusk, in fair weather and in foul, he can experience nature's contrasting moods. By becoming intimate with one locale over the years, if possible, your little one will see that the natural world changes with time—a lesson about change and continuity that he may carry to adulthood.

The web of life

No doubt you will want your child to gain some understanding of how all living things are connected, how they are inextricably dependent on one another for survival. You might tell her that the oxygen in the air you breathe comes from the green plants around her, and that for there always to be new plants, their flowers must be pollinated by insects or by the wind. Scientists call the sum total of nature's dependencies the web of life. The belief that what affects one strand in the web ultimately affects the whole is the basis of ecology.

Outdoor etiquette

The foundation of wilderness etiquette is simple: Do not leave your mark upon nature. This means:

- Hike only on trails. If your family must venture off, walk in single file to minimize damage to plant life.
- Never litter; carry trash home or deposit it in park receptacles.
- Read posted rules and follow them exactly.
- When in doubt about an activity on protected lands, ask permission.
- If you must collect specimens, check first for permission, then concentrate on abundant species, taking just a few of each. Use scissors to avoid damaging plants' stems and roots. Never carve on tree trunks.
- Do not disturb animals. Lift logs and rocks carefully to observe the life under them and put them back as you found them. Examine only one or two per hike.
- Avoid loud noises.

The concept of the web is a rather lofty notion for a small child to grasp, probably too abstract for even the brightest preschooler. You can, however, introduce the idea to your youngster by pointing out food chains, which are strands in the web. One simple food chain starts with a caterpillar munching on a leaf. The caterpillar is eaten by a bird; the bird by a small mammal. If your child does not catch a glimpse of several of the links in this chain in the wild, you both can look for a book that illustrates the principle or find examples in your garden or local park. No doubt she will have lots of questions, so be prepared to give appropriate answers.

Conservation
On your outings, your youngster will probably acquire both a feeling for the importance of conservation and a respect for nature unconsciously, watching you treat animals and plants with reverence and care. You can foster good habits by mentioning that wilderness plants and animals have the same need for gentle treatment as he has. When planning activities, be sure to observe wilderness etiquette *(box, opposite)*. And should you see an abuse, such as litter, get your child to help tidy up— and explain why. This is important. Be sure, of course, always to praise his efforts.

To enhance his wilderness experience, this boy is packing a few pieces of useful equipment, including binoculars, apparatus for collecting insects and plants, and a field guide.

Sharpening the senses
Although young children are naturally alert and curious, much about the teeming and vibrant wilderness environment may escape your child's notice until it is brought to his attention. As you hike in a shadowy forest or enjoy a walk along a beach, get him to focus on aspects of the passing scene—a pine cone dangling from a tree, perhaps, or a starfish washed up on the sand. Ask him to listen and sniff, to run his hand over tree bark, to peer beneath a fern frond or rock. Through such simple observations he can construct his own web of connectedness. ∴

Woodlands and Fields

Woodlands and fields lure child and grown-up alike. Forests contain hidden worlds, while open fields display their treasures. Encourage your child to unlock the secrets of these wonderlands. In both, constant change alters the web of life, and to survive, the creatures that live there must use their adaptations. Even a newly fallen branch can present an occasion to talk about the reclusive animals that will seek shelter and food within it or under it.

You need few excuses to wander with your youngster through a deciduous forest, where trees shed their leaves annually. Expect to get waylaid, however, by the active world underfoot. The ground itself teems with burrowing and crawling creatures—earthworms, millipedes, snails, slugs, spiders. Some feed on decaying leaves, some on one another. You may sight such woodland vegetarians as mice and rabbits nibbling flowers and other soft-stemmed plants, but you can also play wildlife detective with your child, examining twigs and nuts for tooth marks left by squirrels, chipmunks, and voles.

There is another kind of woodland you might profitably visit: a coniferous forest, where evergreen trees dominate. Stroll through the dense stands, listen to the quiet, and smell the air sharp with the scent of resin. Many of the insects in coniferous forests bore into twigs, needles, and wood for food and to lay eggs. The red ant makes its home in plain view on the forest floor. If you and your young one spot a large mound of pine needles—possibly as large as five feet high and ten feet in diameter—you may be onto a nest of red ants, which devour insects that feed on and destroy timber. But be careful: Red ants bite when disturbed.

At the edge of many woods, you may happen on a field of grasses and wildflowers, often where land has been cleared and vegetation has grown over it. On these open tracts, your youngster will get an especially good view of active food chains, for insects are readily observed feeding on the plants, and birds feeding on the insects in turn. Visit a meadow at night, too, taking along a strong flashlight covered with red cellophane to create a tinted beam that will not startle the resident wildlife. Thus equipped, you are likely to see moths hovering over the pale flowers and earthworms poking above the ground, in search of food and mates.

In such environments, numerous other opportunities for special activities abound: bird-watching, taking rubbings of tree bark, collecting natural artifacts such as leaves and seed pods *(pages 104-109),* or looking for animal hideouts. On the following pages you will find suggestions for the kinds of projects that a visit with your child to a field or woods is bound to spark.

Exploring autumn

Enjoying an invigorating autumn ramble, this collector adds yet another colorful leaf to his bounty. Give your child a plastic bag to keep leaves fresh and challenge him to see how many kinds he can pick up. If he is old enough, ask him to describe their colors, shapes, and textures. Take a look, too, at various seeds and pods—milkweed, for instance, and the satiny floss inside.

Texture, contour, and fine detail emerge as the leaf collector makes a leaf print at home. For an easy rubbing method, have your child place a hard, thick-veined leaf between two pieces of strong, thin paper. Then have him rub the paper with the side of a crayon, thick pencil, or graphite stick to make a lasting record of the leaf's outline and veins.

After pinning a leaf to a piece of paper on cardboard, the boy flicks a toothbrush dipped in tempera paint with a pencil to spatter the leaf's surface. When the leaf is removed, it will leave its silhouette behind. Alternatively, he could paint directly on the leaf with a brush, using short outward strokes to keep the paint from seeping underneath, from just inside to just outside the edges of the leaf.

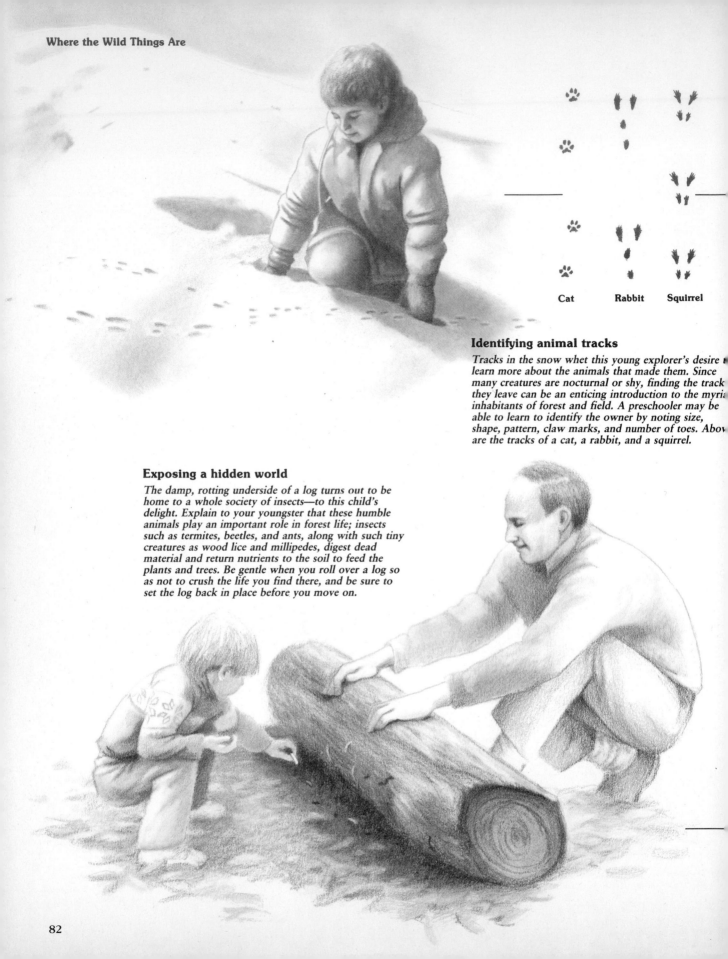

| Cat | Rabbit | Squirrel |

Identifying animal tracks

*Tracks in the snow whet this young explorer's desire t
learn more about the animals that made them. Since
many creatures are nocturnal or shy, finding the track
they leave can be an enticing introduction to the myri
inhabitants of forest and field. A preschooler may be
able to learn to identify the owner by noting size,
shape, pattern, claw marks, and number of toes. Abov
are the tracks of a cat, a rabbit, and a squirrel.*

Exposing a hidden world

*The damp, rotting underside of a log turns out to be
home to a whole society of insects—to this child's
delight. Explain to your youngster that these humble
animals play an important role in forest life; insects
such as termites, beetles, and ants, along with such tiny
creatures as wood lice and millipedes, digest dead
material and return nutrients to the soil to feed the
plants and trees. Be gentle when you roll over a log so
as not to crush the life you find there, and be sure to
set the log back in place before you move on.*

Crafting a nest

Constructing a bird nest gives a youngster insight into a wild creature's home. On a nature walk with your child, look closely at nests, then collect similar materials from the undergrowth and forest floor. At home, have your youngster form a modeling-dough mixture into a basic nest shape; she can then stick any bark, twigs, leaves, grasses, and moss she may have gathered into it, creating her own nest—and in the process gaining an appreciation of the instinct that guides a bird to build a snug home for the young it is going to raise.

Collecting bones

Young hikers reassemble the skeleton of a forest creature they stumbled upon on an outing. Bones like these are generally found in early spring in undisturbed areas, after the lean winter months. They should be collected and bagged with a stick or gloves. Avoid touching them with your bare hands until they are clean. You can whiten and disinfect them by soaking them overnight in a solution of three parts water and one part bleach. Together, you and your youngster can use a guidebook to identify the owner of the bones.

Studying a bird home

Pointing to an abandoned nest, this boy will remove it and take it home to display on a shelf. Since most bird nests are used for one season only, there is no harm in taking an obviously deserted one from its perch in late fall. Search for nests at the edge of forests, where birds often roost, and wear gloves to protect your hands from any biting insects that might be present. Place the nest in a sealed box with mothballs for two weeks to rid it of pests. As your child examines the nest, he will probably discover everything from moss to string; explain to him that birds scavenge widely for building materials, drawing upon both natural and human-made sources.

Observing a snake

Encouraged to examine a garden-variety snake close up, these children marvel at its sleekness. Most snakes are not venomous (pages 136-137). On a day trip with your child, you may spot one skimming through the grass or leaves. To pick it up, hold it securely behind the head and support the rest of its body, being careful not to let it dangle from your hands.

Sprouting a pair of socks

A child expresses wonderment as tiny seeds sprout from his socks (left). For a homegrown meadow of your own, outfit your little one in heavy, high, wool socks and go tramping through a field in late summer or early fall, when ripe seeds will get caught in the fibers (above). Remove the socks, place them in a shallow dish or pan, and soak them with water. Explain to your child that each seed contains all the ingredients and parts necessary to produce a plant just like the one from which it came. Place the socks in a sunny window and keep them moist. In about a week, the seeds will sprout. The project will give you a chance to discuss ways seeds are transported—traveling on the wind, carried by animal fur, dropped by birds.

Inspecting pollen

Peering into a flower with the aid of a magnifying glass, a youngster observes tiny pollen grains on its delicate stamens. Explain to your child that these grains help plants form seeds. The bright petals attract insects, which feed on its sweet nectar, inadvertently picking up pollen grains and transporting them to other flowers, where cross-pollination occurs.

Netting insects

Sweeping an open field with large nets, two children scoop up meadow inhabitants for study. After your youngster has learned to net insects on the ground, show her how to catch flying insects. Carefully shake the contents into a jar so she can examine her catch, which may include everything from grasshoppers, beetles, crickets, and spiders to perhaps even a butterfly, then release the insects when she is through.

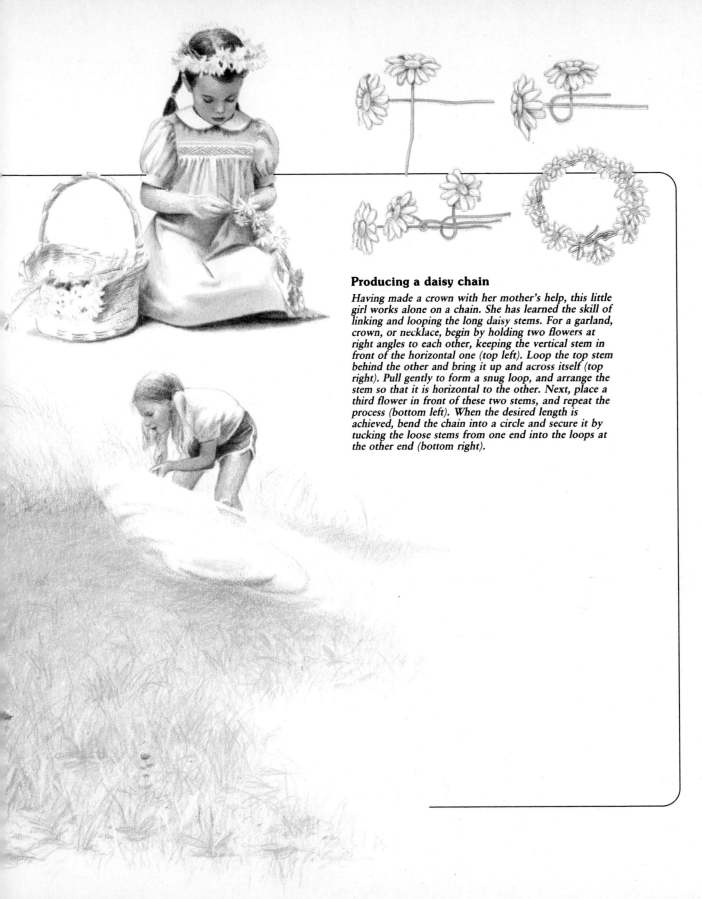

Producing a daisy chain

Having made a crown with her mother's help, this little girl works alone on a chain. She has learned the skill of linking and looping the long daisy stems. For a garland, crown, or necklace, begin by holding two flowers at right angles to each other, keeping the vertical stem in front of the horizontal one (top left). Loop the top stem behind the other and bring it up and across itself (top right). Pull gently to form a snug loop, and arrange the stem so that it is horizontal to the other. Next, place a third flower in front of these two stems, and repeat the process (bottom left). When the desired length is achieved, bend the chain into a circle and secure it by tucking the loose stems from one end into the loops at the other end (bottom right).

Freshwater Realms

Dabbling at the edge of a pond or stream is an activity that appeals greatly to children. The gooey mud itself is a never-failing attraction, and the wildlife on the banks and in the water easily captures and holds youthful imaginations. Marshes are exciting for youngsters to visit, too, especially in spring and fall, when huge flocks of migrating ducks and geese descend to feed.

Tiny ponds, rushing streams and rivers, quiet wetlands—all have lessons to give your child. Indeed, her love of novelty will flourish in these freshwater habitats. For animals and plants often have special and sometimes exotic features that enable them to survive the particular challenges of their aquatic environment. Once you begin to point these out—the water lily's floating leaf, the duck's "raincoat" of oily feathers, the frog's webbed feet, the crayfish's armor—your child will recognize such adaptations and bring them to your attention herself.

Walking together along a stream or riverbank, you might ask your youngster how she thinks the plants and animals stay in place as swift currents flow by. Or take a close look at the plants growing along the water's edge, and see how they attach themselves to half-exposed rocks and roots. The caddis fly constructs a shelter for itself from gravel and tiny twigs, glued together with a sticky secretion that anchors the shelter to stones or the stream bottom. Larger animals in fast water display other kinds of adaptations; the beaver's broad tail and webbed feet, for example, help power it through riffles and rapids.

In the quieter waters of a gentle brook or pond or along the banks, you may find frogs and turtles—creatures that rely on both land and water for their survival. On the water itself, you may sight water striders that lightly dance across its surface on spidery legs or diving beetles that hold bubbles of air against their bodies so they can breathe when they descend to feed or lay eggs. Ask your youngster to consider the special problems of finding shelter in the water. If a pond is shallow, wade out with her to look for tiny organisms, such as snails or flatworms, that may be hiding on the underside of a water lily's broad pad.

Wetlands—swamps, marshes, and bogs—are a whole other world. At a cypress swamp, a youngster will see one way the plant world copes with constantly wet roots: Cypress trees have broad, flared bases that help brace them, enabling them to stand upright in soggy soil without toppling over. Marshes are generally covered with flexible, leafy plants—grasses, rushes, sedges, wildflowers, cattails—that thrive in water and sunlight and provide cover and often food for snakes, mammals, birds, and their young. Here you and your child may have the good fortune to spot a great blue heron, a bird whose gangly legs and arched neck enable it to fish in shallow water without getting its feathers wet.

Most likely, since the animals living in such a habitat are as shy as any other wild creatures, such glimpses will be from a distance. Still, as the next pages will show, there is also a great deal of life for your young naturalist to explore close up in freshwater communities.

Checking out a mussel's home

A hinged mussel shell offers a couple of curious children a chance to glimpse the inside of a mollusk's armor. Mussels can move about the soft bottom of ponds, quiet streams, lakes, or rivers, but most of the time they remain still, filtering particles of food from water. Shells found broken open on the bank have probably been left there by hungry opossums or raccoons feeding on the contents.

Making a water scope

Before leaving on an expedition, a boy and his mother put the final touches on a water scope, which will help them more easily view pond life by reducing distortion due to ripples. To make this instrument, remove both ends of a half-gallon milk or orange-juice carton. Cover one end with plastic wrap; secure it snugly with a heavy rubber band (below, left). At the pond's edge, have your child gently put the plastic-covered end into quiet water and peer through it at the plants and animals beneath the surface (below, right).

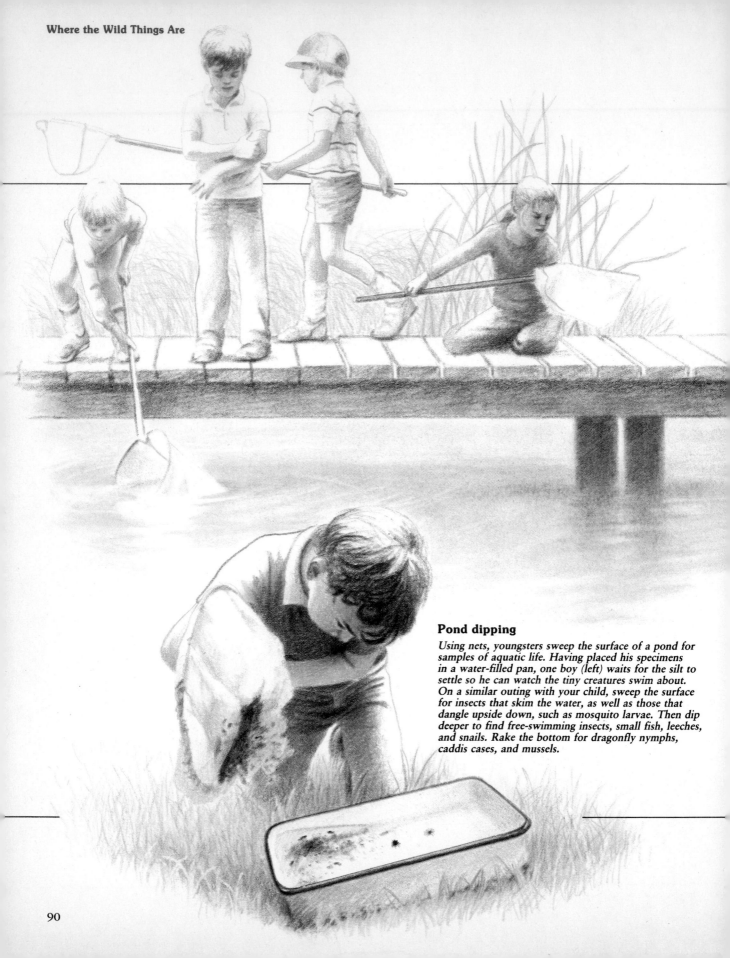

Pond dipping

Using nets, youngsters sweep the surface of a pond for samples of aquatic life. Having placed his specimens in a water-filled pan, one boy (left) waits for the silt to settle so he can watch the tiny creatures swim about. On a similar outing with your child, sweep the surface for insects that skim the water, as well as those that dangle upside down, such as mosquito larvae. Then dip deeper to find free-swimming insects, small fish, leeches, and snails. Rake the bottom for dragonfly nymphs, caddis cases, and mussels.

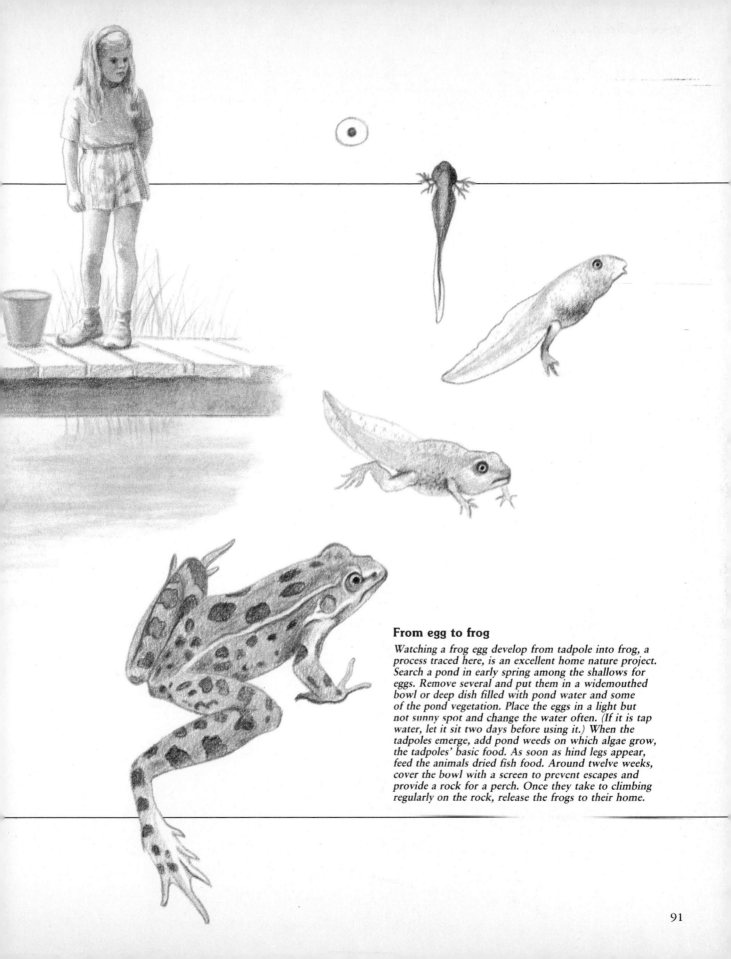

From egg to frog

Watching a frog egg develop from tadpole into frog, a process traced here, is an excellent home nature project. Search a pond in early spring among the shallows for eggs. Remove several and put them in a widemouthed bowl or deep dish filled with pond water and some of the pond vegetation. Place the eggs in a light but not sunny spot and change the water often. (If it is tap water, let it sit two days before using it.) When the tadpoles emerge, add pond weeds on which algae grow, the tadpoles' basic food. As soon as hind legs appear, feed the animals dried fish food. Around twelve weeks, cover the bowl with a screen to prevent escapes and provide a rock for a perch. Once they take to climbing regularly on the rock, release the frogs to their home.

Visitors from the Wild

Tending a wild animal at home can enhance a child's understanding of the animal and its needs. Designing a suitable environment teaches a youngster that the animal exists best in a certain physical surrounding. And caring for it will encourage a sense of nurturing—and instill good conservation habits. Although your child may become delightfully attached to her wild friend, return it to its habitat in about a week. Explain that an animal lives best in its own home.

With some practice, you can catch reptiles and amphibians. First, however, you need to decide what type of animal interests your child and consult a field guide to make sure you look for a species that is neither harmful nor rare. Remember, too, that most parks do not allow the taking of wildlife.

To minimize the animal's discomfort, you should prepare its temporary home in advance. The environment you create should be as close to the animal's natural habitat as possible; to keep the captive from escaping, use a ventilated lid on your tank. Readying the environment beforehand will also give you a chance to talk with your youngster about the responsibility of caring for a wild creature. Tell her that the animal is self-sufficient in its natural environment, but that once taken from there it will depend on her for food and water. And be prepared to offer plenty of help; a small child cannot assume the responsibility alone.

Below are some animals to keep as visitors, along with notes on their special needs. You may want to check with a zoo, nature center, or pet store, as well, to learn more about how to catch and care for wild creatures. Above all, encourage your child to handle her ward gently, with the same kind of respect that you give her.

Water turtles and bullfrogs adjust well to a ten-gallon glass tank, such as the one shown here. Scatter fine gravel over the bottom and half fill the tank with water; put a large rock in the center for the captive to climb on to bask. This tank has a sliding top with narrow ventilation slits. Turtles and frogs will feed on live backyard insects and worms; turtles also eat fleshy fruits and vegetables. Preferences may vary, so if your visitor ignores the fare, try another item.

Toads are comfortable in woodsy and land-water habitats. For an environment similar to the one illustrated here, layer soil and leaves on the bottom of a ten-gallon tank and add a small log for the toad to rest on. Use the same type of sliding top as described above. Provide a shallow dish of water, and offer live insects and worms for food. Tell your child to handle the toad carefully, because its skin is fragile.

For housing a snake, prepare a wood-and-mesh enclosure, which will be cooler than a glass tank; cover it with a tightly fitting mesh lid and place it out of direct sunlight. Many snakes live in relatively dry environments, but do make water available for sipping and soaking. In the wild, snakes often retreat behind rocks, so include a suitable hiding place. Because this captive is a tree snake, a branch has been provided. Consult a reptile guide to find out what your specimen's dietary requirements are.

Handling a turtle

Holding a slider water turtle on its side for a close look, children see defensive behavior at work. The turtle reacts to their handling, as all other turtles do when they sense danger, by drawing in its head and legs. Your child may safely handle most kinds of turtles, but it is a good idea for him to wash his hands afterward— as he should do after touching any wild animal.

Preparing a nesting box

At the end of winter, a wood-duck nesting box in a frozen pond stands empty, as this girl has discovered. With her father, she will clear out the old nest and pile fresh wood shavings inside. The wood duck, frequently spotted near tree-ringed ponds and lakes and in swampy areas, does not construct its own home, but searches out natural cavities or boxes to lay its eggs. If you live near enough to the wood duck's habitat to tend a nesting box in spring, you might want to construct one yourself and "adopt" a duck.

The Magic Place between Water and Land

Spacious beaches, pungent air, the roar of waves—is it any wonder that seashores stir the senses, fuel a child's fantasy life, and inspire him to dig for treasure? Here, where the water flows back and forth in ceaseless rhythm, many creatures make their home. A child's penchant for detective work comes richly into play once he finds out that many dwellers in or near the intertidal zone—the area that is laid bare each day as the water recedes—are adept at hiding when their domain is bared and that he must search diligently if he wants to find them.

On the great sand beaches along the Atlantic, and on the narrow strips below the rocks on the Pacific coast, live many burrowing creatures—lugworms, small clams, buglike crustaceans. Often the only evidence that they are there are tiny holes dimpling the beach's wet smoothness or small, sandy heaps—the trash piles left after lugworms have filtered nutrients from the sand. Encourage your youngster to dig quickly to glimpse a burrower; if you teach him to follow the retreating waves, he may see pale troops of mole crabs chasing the tide. During peak tides each May and June along the Atlantic coast all the way from Maine to Florida, he might even be fortunate enough to behold an extraordinary drama as hundreds of horseshoe crabs come crawling ashore to lay their eggs.

Tides also determine the extent of animal domains on rocky shores, such as those of northern New England. Where the surf provides a constant spray, you will find colonies of barnacles, which are close relatives of crabs, and limpets, a kind of snail. Prowl the intertidal zone, looking for pools left in crevices when the tide recedes, and you will discover entire communities of marine creatures living there: starfish, sea anemones, small fish, perhaps a hermit crab. And atop exposed boulders and stones in the water, you will probably find flourishing seaweeds—tough, slippery marine algae. See if you and your little one can pull off a piece to examine the fingerlike projections that anchored it to the rock.

In some Atlantic coastal areas, where there are protective barrier islands, another type of seashore environment may intrigue a small child. At the edge of quiet bays and inlets, sediment builds up and supports tall grasses. Since the barrier islands deter the brunt of the ocean waves and tides, some animals stay aboveground. You may see scores of fiddler crabs digging in the mud, or dozens of saltwater mussels clustered near the grasses.

So that your youngster's experience at the seashore can be the fullest one possible, the following pages contain suggestions for a variety of activities that will help fix in his mind forever the water world.

Combing the high-tide line

A young beachcomber forages the strand line of a smooth, sandy shore for shells, driftwood, sea glass, horseshoe crab shells, and pieces of seaweed. Beachcombing is best after a storm's heavy surf washes debris from the ocean floor. At home your budding naturalist may enjoy identifying his finds and arranging them by category or assembling a free-form sculpture or collage to hang on his bedroom wall (pages 108-109).

A salty experiment

To show your child that ocean salt and table salt are the same substance, put seawater one-half inch deep in a wide-rimmed dish (far left) and leave it in the sun for a day or two. Bring the dish indoors at night to keep it from gathering dew. Eventually the water will evaporate, leaving salt crystals behind (near left). You might set a small dish of table salt next to the sea salt; ask your child to put a bit of each on his tongue to find out if there is any difference in taste.

Casting animal tracks

Indoors on a rainy day at the beach, a mother shows her daughter how to take a sand casting of an animal track, in this case their dog's paw. To make a similar cast, you need a shallow box placed in a tray, water, and plaster of Paris. Half fill the box with sand and dampen it, then press into it whatever you wish to cast—perhaps a seashell or a sand dollar. Now mix the plaster and fill the impression left behind when you removed the object. Let the plaster dry, then turn out the cast. Brush off any sand and the cast is ready.

Meeting a lobster face to face

A father holds up a lobster for his son to study, pointing out that instead of having bones inside, it wears its skeleton outside, using it for protection. As the lobster grows bigger, it outgrows its shell, shedding it and developing a new one. To study a live lobster, you will probably have to purchase one. Be sure that its claws are held shut with a thick rubber band or tape. Explain to your child that the lobster uses the heavy claw for crushing prey and the light one for cutting it into bite-size portions.

Crabbing

Flushed with success, a mother and son hoist their catch, a green crab. They will put it in a bucket to examine it and then return it to the sea. To catch a crab of your own, tie one end of a string to a stick and the other to a bit of chicken or shellfish and drop the bait in shallow water, near rocks and weeds. When you have caught your crab, scoop it up with a net. Be sure to check local regulations concerning crabbing.

Making a fish print

This little girl shows off her Japanese-looking fish print. So that your child can make one of her own, choose a fish with well-defined scales and wash and dry it. Give her a wide, soft brush and have her paint one side of the fish with food coloring. Next have her lay a sheet of paper over the fish and press down on it, rubbing gently to pick up an impression of the whole body, including fins and tail. Stretch the paper flat and leave it to dry. Repeat the process once or twice without repainting the fish; the second print may be clearer.

Watching and feeding shorebirds

With bread and crackers for a lure, a little girl attracts a flock of gulls. These sharp-eyed scavengers find beach and shallows rewarding hunting grounds; they will peck at everything from clams to discarded hot dogs. Your child will have fun watching such other seashore inhabitants as plovers, terns, and sanderlings as they follow the surf in search of food. She might also enjoy scanning the sky with binoculars. And if she gazes at the ocean some distance out, she may be able to spot a leaping fish or even a dolphin or two.

The Varied Desert

To the eyes of a child unfamiliar with the desert, such an arid landscape might at first appear lifeless. She will soon find, however, that the desert supports all manner of living things. Desert animals and plants have developed marvelous adaptations to this dry and sometimes windy environment. And the desert can show a brighter face, too. If she is fortunate enough to visit in the spring, after adequate rainfall, she may see a carpet of wildflowers or the blooms of the prickly cacti.

Most desert areas lie in the western United States, but their terrains and wildlife vary widely. In Utah, for example, you will see red-rock cliffs, arches, and canyons. Elsewhere, you may find hillsides covered with gray-green sagebrush; in a few places you will pass stretches of sand and flowing dunes. In most of Arizona, on the other hand, the desert is dotted with cacti, shrubs, and trees and harbors many species of wildlife.

In the southwestern deserts, your child may learn a great deal about how plants and animals survive high temperatures and sporadic rainfall. Examine some cacti with her. They lack leaves, since leaves would require too much water to support. Instead, they have spines, which, among other things, help shield them from sun and moisture-robbing winds. Many cacti, such as the famous saguaro found in most of the Sonoran desert, are deeply furrowed; the pleats expand as the plant absorbs rainwater and contract during dry spells. Explain to your child that these slow-growing cacti also provide shelter for many animals; she may be thrilled to see animal holes or sight the creatures that nest in the saguaro's walls—the Gila woodpecker or the elf owl.

Rain, heat, and the land itself control the lives of many desert animals. After a summer downpour, for example, you might be able to spot scores of spadefoot toads, which have suddenly surfaced to lay eggs in temporary pools. To help them cope with the sun, some desert creatures have larger-than-usual body parts that radiate heat; thus the jackrabbit displays very large ears. And in a world with few places to hide, the kangaroo rat has long hind legs that allow it to bound away from predators.

As you venture out to explore the desert with your child, carry plenty of water and dress suitably. Explore in the cooler early morning hours and at dusk, when more creatures are about. Use common sense: Note where you are going, be observant at all times, and watch where you sit and put your hands. If you begin your trek at one of the many desert parks, you will have the benefit of the park staff's expertise. With their guidance—and the suggestions on these pages—your young naturalist should be able to absorb many of the lessons of this unusual realm.

Exploring a petrified forest

A mother and daughter trace rings of growth in a fossilized tree (left). An amazing sight, these stone fossils of toppled ancient trees are scattered throughout the Petrified Forest National Park, in eastern Arizona. You might briefly explain to your child that millions of years ago trees died and were buried beneath layers of earth. When the landscape changed and they were exposed once more, they had turned to stone.

Rock research

A budding geologist cracks open a rock, looking for unusual patterns, textures, or colors—or perhaps even a fossil. To crack a rock, first wrap it in cloth so chips will not fly (right); then strike it with a hammer. If you plan to gather rocks to take home, check first to see whether this is permitted in the area you are exploring.

Painting with sand

Sprinkling colored sand onto cardboard, a little girl creates a desert-inspired design. For this activity, put a small amount of fine sand in each of several jars, add a little food coloring, and shake. Spread the sand on newspaper and let it dry; then poke holes in the lids to form shakers, put the sand back in the jars, and screw on the lids. Help your child paint glue on the cardboard so the sand will stick, and then let her go to town.

Attracting nocturnal animals

Since many desert creatures wait until the cool of the night to feed and drink, a mother and son create a water hole for some local denizens to visit. While he scatters grain as a lure (below), she smooths the sand so the animals' tracks will show. Sticks placed across the pool will allow any insects that fall in to crawl out. Your child will enjoy this activity, especially the early morning return to compare the tracks with those shown in a guide or on a chart like the one opposite.

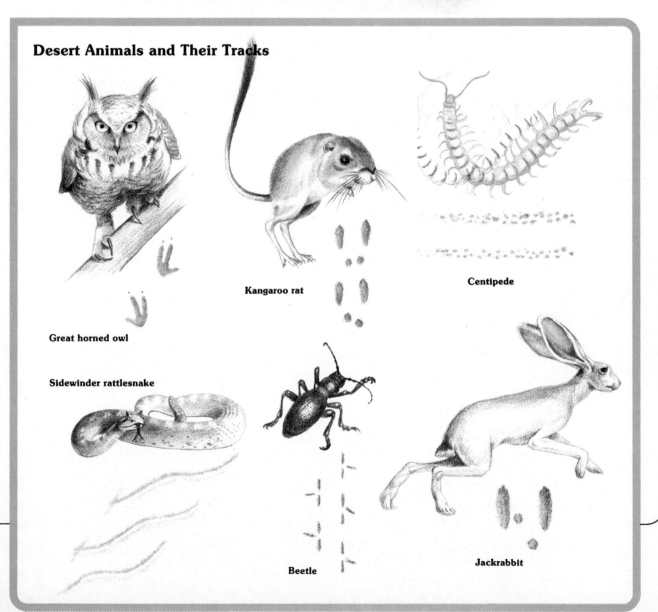

Desert Animals and Their Tracks

Great horned owl

Kangaroo rat

Centipede

Sidewinder rattlesnake

Beetle

Jackrabbit

Preserving and Displaying Collections

Evolving a Sense of Order

When your child empties his pockets after a day at the beach or a walk in the woods, you probably see a heap of nature's castoffs—empty seed pods, abandoned shells, molted feathers. With a little organizing, some simple equipment, and your guidance, your child can become a real collector, and his hodgepodge can grow into an interesting, informative, and beautiful nature collection.

Many young collectors gather items in one category, such as seed pods, leaves, or rocks. But yours may as likely decide to collect by color—only red things, for example, from red seashells to red wildflowers to autumn's flaming maple leaves. Or he may choose to display only items picked up on a single day's ramble. Any of these approaches can teach your little collector a good deal about the natural world, about handling fragile objects, and about observing, categorizing, and researching.

On trips, you can encourage your child's collecting by pointing out suitable natural objects, such as pine cones, snail shells, water-smoothed rocks. You may also need to provide the boxes, bags, and jars that are so handy for collecting and storing natural objects. It is up to you as the adult, of course, to see whether collecting is permitted and to obtain permission to do so where necessary. You must also consult field guides to see that nothing your youngster collects is rare—or poisonous *(page 139)*.

For divided containers in which your child can sort and display his collection, you can save empty egg cartons, and your supermarket can give you molded cardboard fruit-crate dividers *(page 108)*. You and your youngster might assemble several empty matchboxes—or cut off the bottoms of a few milk cartons, leaving a one-inch rim—to serve as compartments when set in cigar boxes or shoebox lids. Have ready scissors, tweezers, and white glue—they may be pressed into service. Tape, ribbon or seam binding, and string are also useful.

One of the most breathtaking, and most popular, of all displays is a butterfly collection, mounted like the one below. With your help and a few special tools, your young collector can mount his specimens as lepidopterists do.

Live specimens should be asphyxiated in a killing jar *(opposite)* to minimize damage to their wings. A dead specimen with its wings stiffly upright should be treated in a relaxing jar so that the wing joints regain flexibility. A freshly killed (or newly relaxed) specimen is then fastened to a spreading board to dry, with its wings outspread, before being mounted on a display board *(below)*. Spreading boards are available from biological supply companies; if you want to make your own, glue two strips of cork tile or plastic foam to a board, leaving a groove between them as wide as a butterfly's thorax.

To prepare the killing jar (above, left), put a few drops of nail-polish remover on a ball of crumpled tissue paper, drop it into a widemouthed jar, and cover it with a layer of dry tissue paper. Put the live specimen in the jar and cover the jar tightly. After three hours, use tweezers to remove the specimen. In a relaxing jar (above, right), the relaxing agent is humidity, provided by a layer of wet sand. To keep specimens clean, cover the sand with a dry jar lid. With the jar tightly covered, relaxing a rigid specimen takes several days.

To fasten a specimen to the spreading board, first push a straight pin through the thorax, lay the thorax in the spreading board's groove, and press the pin into the groove. Then lay a strip of paper over one pair of wings, top to bottom, and pin it at both ends. Secure the other pair of wings with a second paper strip. Set the board in a warm, dry place for two weeks, with mothball chips nearby to repel insects. To remove the dried specimen, unpin the paper strips, then lift the specimen by the pin through its thorax.

Choose a thick piece of plastic foam for a mounting board. Show your child how to use a pair of tweezers to position the specimens, and how to secure each butterfly with the straight pin.

Five Easy Ways to Keep Plant Materials

Once they have been collected, leaves and flowers perish quickly if they are not preserved. This can be done successfully using any of the five simple methods on these pages.

To ensure a harvest of blooms and foliage that will not mold, cut plants with scissors during the warmest part of a sunny day and put them into a plastic bag. Being careful to keep the bag out of direct sunlight to minimize wilting, begin working on the plants immediately.

The preserving methods shown here are easy, and most rely on simple household supplies. The only unusual materials are glycerin, found in drugstores, and sterilized sand, available from garden-supply shops. Your choice of method depends partly on your plant material *(opposite)*, and partly on the purpose your child has in mind for the specimens. A plant gathered whole for later study is best pressed flat or sand-dried, since its foliage would wither if it were air-dried.

Ask what your child would like to do with his preserved plants afterward. He may want to use them in artwork, display them as they are, or collaborate with you to arrange them in a vase for a bouquet that lasts all winter.

Air drying: a natural look for small flowers

On your expeditions, you and your child can search for the long-stemmed, small-headed flowers suitable for air drying, the simplest preserving method. Good candidates include daisies, black-eyed Susans, and goldenrod. Strip the leaves from the stalks and tie the stalks in bunches of ten or fewer as soon as you get them home. Hang them upside down in a dark, dry place for about a week.

Sand drying: holding large flowers' shapes

Sand drying preserves the shapes of foliage such as ivy and of larger flower heads, such as columbine, Queen Anne's lace, and sunflowers. Start with a one-inch layer of sterilized sand in a shoebox. Leave a half-inch stem on each flower head or leaf, and embed each one face up in the sand. Gently cover with a one-inch layer of sand. After seven to ten days, pour the sand slowly out of the box and shake the dried plant material.

Mounting a leaf collage in wax paper

Lay a sheet of wax paper on a towel-covered heat-resistant surface and let your child arrange a few flat leaves on it. Lay another sheet of wax paper over the collage, cover the assembly with another towel, and glide a warm iron over it. The wax will melt, penetrating and preserving the leaves and fusing the sheets of paper together. After you trim the uneven edges, your child will enjoy hanging his collage in a window where the light can shine through it.

Pressing plants to dry them flat

Pressing is best for leaves that are already fairly flat and for small spring wildflowers. Begin with a thick layer of newspaper. Cover it with a paper towel, lay a few leaves or plants out flat, then cover them with another paper towel and more newspaper. Repeat for more layers. Top the stack with a heavy book and leave it in a warm, dry place for about three weeks. Take care in removing the dried materials; they may be brittle.

Infusing leaves with glycerin

Allowing fresh autumn leaves to absorb glycerin will preserve some of their colors while changing others. To start the process, mix a solution of two parts water to one part glycerin. Show your child how to crush the stem ends with a hammer (right); this will speed the absorption of the glycerin. Stand the leaves in the glycerin solution for several days. When done, the leaves will stay colorful indefinitely.

The Intrinsic Value of Displaying Collections

After a few collecting expeditions, as your child's hoard of natural objects begins to grow, he will want to show off his trove. Some clever ways of exhibiting collections appear on these pages. As the pictures make clear, a display need not be elaborate or expensive to be effective.

Displaying a collection also brings your youngster new opportunities to develop various aspects of himself, as he handles, compares, appraises, and discusses his finds. Closeup examination sharpens his powers of observation. In thinking about how to situate an object—whether as part of a collage or in a display—he is called on not only to observe intently but also to ponder the item's features, and then make a decision. Each of these provides good practice for the future.

You can help further develop these skills by asking your youngster some questions about aspects of his collection. Once he is invited to discuss texture, shape, color, size, and smell, he will begin to notice and comment on more and more details.

If he has made a collage of things he found all in one place, you can ask him to compare and contrast the various types of items that are included. And in his eagerness to tell you about his observations, he will be developing and sharpening his communication skills as well, learning how to express himself more and more accurately.

Another vital skill that is stimulated by collecting is the ability to classify. Children find great satisfaction in displaying items all belonging to the same class—a rock collection, say, or a shell collection. But classifying objects by other attributes can also be very satisfying. Suggest to your child that he borrow from his collection to make a smaller, temporary display—one in which everything is round, perhaps, or smooth or brown or tiny. You might also suggest that he reorganize his entire collection by a new rule. If it is now arranged according to shape, for example, suggest that he put it in size order or match items according to color.

An artistic exhibit of beach treasures

Attractively arranged on a weathered driftwood board and secured with white glue, a child's collection of natural objects from the beach makes an outstanding collage. This assembly contains crab carapaces, Atlantic moon shells, a mussel shell with a barnacle attached, and jingle and clam shells.

A cataloged rock collection

Each specimen in this neatly arranged rock collection nestles in its own numbered hollow in a cardboard fruit-crate divider. With your help, your preschooler may enjoy using a pocket guide to identify his finds, number them, and list their names. The owner of this collection has also brought out the colors of some of the specimens with a light coating of cooking oil.

Revealing the gemlike colors of sea glass

Rounded, colorful pieces of sea glass, displayed in a jar of water, catch the sunlight on a bright windowsill. These shards of broken bottles, which have tumbled about in the sandy surf until they have lost their sharp edges and shiny surfaces, are a favorite beach collectible with many children.

Every feather in its place

The cut edge of a strip of corrugated cardboard presents a regular series of holes that are just right for a child's collection of feathers. Pinned or taped to the wall, the strip displays the collection while keeping it out of harm's way. This array features elements ranging from a pet parakeet's discarded tail feathers to a peacock feather found on the ground at the zoo.

Mounting a plant collection for wall display

Seam-binding tape provides the holding power in this display of grasses, leaves, and reeds. Fold the ends of the tapes to keep them from fraying, stretch them taut, and pin them to a sheet of posterboard in a diagonal crisscross pattern. Fasten the posterboard to a piece of corkboard, and then let your youngster slip dried plants under the strips of tape.

4

The Joys of Family Camping

Many are the ways a family can enjoy itself, and one of them is roving through the great outdoors. A few days together far from the intrusions of civilization can work wonders for the spirit and create the kind of memories that you and your child will cherish forever. And with each successive outing, you will have opportunities to make new discoveries and share new adventures.

The question is when to start. Only you know when your child is ready to be an agreeable outdoor companion. Some parents begin by hiking, canoeing, bicycling, or cross-country skiing when their child is still a baby; others wait until school age. Most families begin with short day trips, but if you and your spouse are experienced campers and have the equipment and know-how, there is nothing to keep you from heading into the wilderness right away. Still, most families save trips to the remote backcountry for when the children are older. On the following pages, you will find many ideas to help your family get under way.

The wilderness is a place of solitude and beauty, a place for quiet talk and silent reflection. Wherever you go, you will find plenty to admire, such as the magnificent field of mountain wildflowers at right. But do not be disappointed if your little one is not always as enthused about some wonder of nature as you are. Children have their own ideas about what is exciting, and these may not always coincide with an adult view. It is perfectly normal, for example, for a five-year-old to be as interested in skimming stones across a pond as in watching a spectacular sunset unfold. What is important is that by being in the wilds together you are laying a foundation for a lifetime of outdoor fun.

Getting Ready for the Great Outdoors

Once you have decided to treat your youngster to an outing, it is all too tempting to take her in hand, slip on a pack, and just go. But whether you are contemplating a day trip to a local woodland or a week-long outing in the wilderness, it is best to resist this temptation and instead devote as much time as necessary to planning your adventure. Planning is particularly important if you are unfamiliar with the outdoors, or if your campcraft skills are limited or rusty. By taking the time for careful preparation now, you can ensure a safe, enjoyable experience that will leave everyone looking forward to another family outing in the near future.

Where to go

Among the first questions you will have to answer are how and where to go. The possibilities are numerous; they range from simple hiking, biking, or cross-country skiing in a nearby park *(pages 118-121)* to more ambitious backpacking and camping treks *(pages 122-129)* and boating or canoeing trips *(pages 130-133)*. Some of these excursions require special equipment *(pages 114-117)*, particular skills, or both. Others call for little more than the desire to go and some up-front preparation, which should include preliminary exercise to prevent sore muscles.

It is wise at the beginning to pick a place close to home rather than drain away much of your little one's enthusiasm on a lengthy car trip. If you can manage to do so, it is a good idea to visit the area beforehand, or at least to use maps and guidebooks to familiarize yourself with the intended route. Look for places with plenty of potential for play and exploration, and remember that parks and nature preserves are usually less crowded on weekdays than on weekends. You may also wish to see whether such basic amenities as toilet facilities are offered.

Using the National Park Service

For many families, the destination of choice is one of the more than 300 historic and natural areas that are operated by the National Park Service. Established in 1872 with the founding of Yellowstone National Park, the Park Service today incorporates a network of trails, scenic highways, monuments, seashores, rivers, battlefield parks, and wildernesses in almost every part of the country. The Park Service can help you plan for your trip by offering advice on what are the best seasons to visit a park, what kind of weather you can expect, what clothing you ought to bring, and the range of facilities available, including special programs and activities planned for children. Many of the national parks offer guided walks, films and lectures, exhibits, books, and demonstrations of wilderness skills. You can always

Assembling a Survival Kit

Even if you plan only a short stay in the wilderness, it is wise to carry a survival kit in addition to your regular camping equipment. The kit should contain the following items:
- Compass
- Area maps in a waterproof container
- Flashlight and spare batteries
- Insect repellent
- Extra food, such as nuts, raisins, bouillon cubes, and candy
- Canteen of extra water
- Water-purification tablets *(box, page 125)*
- Pocketknife
- Hatchet
- Lightweight foil-backed blanket that holds body heat and can be used as a distress signal
- Candle or fire starter
- Matches in a waterproof container
- First-aid kit and booklet
- Nylon cord or rope
- Mirror for signaling
- Whistle

write before your trip and ask to be sent pamphlets and maps. (See page 139 for the address.)

Other sources of information You can also write for information to state parks and tourist boards, as well as to local, regional, and national wilderness organizations or nature centers. Camping-supply stores can also be helpful. Many of them sell topographical maps and guidebooks. And do not forget your local library or bookstore, which can furnish you with how-to books and magazines specializing in all manner of outdoor activities.

Pausing on a hike, a father shows his son how to check their location with a map and compass. Although the child is too young to read the map, he is absorbing skills that will be handy as he grows older.

Starting out small Whatever the activity—hiking, bicycling, cross-country skiing, backpacking, or canoeing—beginners should start modestly. You can gradually extend the intensity and duration of your activity as your youngster grows older and you both become more confident. Alternatively, you might consider joining forces with friends who are more experienced than you or registering for one of the programs organized by an outdoors club in your area.

Even if you have had a lot of experience as a camper, you should take stock of your own physical condition, especially if your little one will need to be carried or will require special care and attention. Keep in mind, too, when you are mapping out an itinerary, that no matter how old your child is, he is not going to be able to cover as much ground as you can, so you will have to allow for frequent stops. Be prepared to make those pauses as interesting as possible, perhaps with a closeup examination of the plants and trees growing in the immediate area. ⋮

What You'll Need to Camp

Buying camping gear for a family can represent a considerable investment. But there is some consolation in the knowledge that, if they are properly cared for, many essential items will last for years. And by starting small and adding new equipment as necessary, you can avoid large up-front outlays. On simple day trips, for example, you need only a daypack or a fanny pack *(opposite, center row)*, a first-aid kit *(page 135)*, and depending upon the age of your child, perhaps a baby carrier *(opposite, bottom row)*.

Some outdoor outfitters rent equipment—an attractive option for first-time campers. Renting allows you to try various items and get a better idea of your family's requirements before making a financial commitment. Many mail-order catalogers stock camping equipment and can offer buying tips, toll-free, over the telephone. Several of these merchants also sell child-size gear and clothing. Look for brightly colored outerwear that will make your child easier to spot in the woods, and for garments with adjustable straps or drawstrings; they may provide an extra year of wear for your rapidly growing child.

Selecting a Tent

Depending on the size of your family, you can opt for a two-person pup tent, a four-person dome tent, or a full-size wall tent *(below)*. Most tents are made of durable, lightweight nylon. Because of the extra comfort it offers, a tent with a separate outer cover, or fly, is usually worth the added cost. The air space between the tent wall and the protective fly acts as insulation, keeping the interior warmer in cold weather, cooler in hot weather.

Test a tent for comfort before you buy. Will the whole family fit, or do you need two tents? Tents with flexible aluminum or fiberglass poles with shock cords (rubber sheathed in nylon) running through the tubes are easier to set up than tents with solid poles. A good tent has reinforced pole pockets, bugproof netting over vents and entrances, and a waterproof floor. Practice setting up the tent at home so that you can erect it easily at a campsite.

Sleeping Bags and Pads

Sleeping bags vary in shape and insulating material. There are two basic shapes, rectangular *(far right)* and mummy *(near right)*. Mummy-shaped bags are less roomy but warmer, since they trap more body heat. A compromise shape, the modified mummy *(right, center)*, has some of the benefits of both styles.

Most bags are rated on the basis of their warmth. Some are suitable for spring, summer, and autumn use, others for year-round camping. Down-filled bags provide the most warmth for their weight. With proper care, a down bag can last up to fifteen years. But they are also expensive and dry slowly after having been rained on; their failure to dry quickly is also something to consider if your child is not yet toilet trained. Wet synthetic-filled bags can be wrung out and still insulate effectively. They have a life span of three to six years.

Sleeping on the ground can be a hard, cold, and damp experience, so you should also consider buying an air mattress or a foam pad to put under your sleeping bag. Look for one with good insulating qualities.

Daypacks

A six-year-old may be able to handle a framepack that is loaded with no more than 25 percent of her body weight. For younger preschoolers or for yourself on day trips, buy a nylon daypack *(near right)* or fanny pack *(far right)*. The more expensive models may have handy exterior pockets, interior compartments, or both. Look for packs with padded, adjustable shoulder straps, self-repairing coil zippers, and sturdy seam stitching. On a daypack, a waist strap can also be a worthwhile feature.

Child Carriers

A good carrier holds your baby securely, leaving your hands free. The soft-fabric sling type *(far right)* is for newborns and tiny infants. It should be washable, have adjustable straps, and provide adequate head support for your precious cargo.

When your baby can hold her head up, use a tubular-frame back carrier *(near right)*. Traditional models have a fabric seat on an aluminum frame. Newer models have a waist belt that takes the strain off the shoulders. Look for a safety belt and padding on the tubing near your baby. The holes for your baby's legs should never be higher than the seat. For your own comfort, make sure there is padding on your shoulder straps.

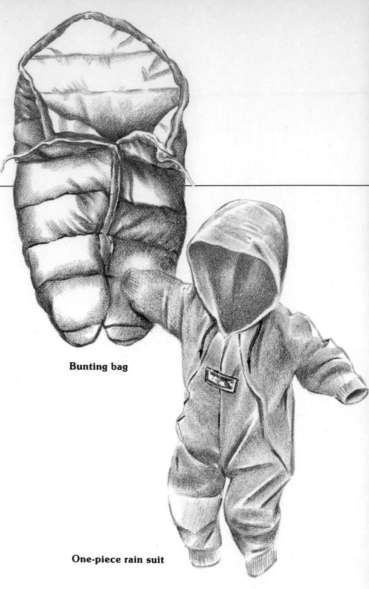

Clothing and Footwear for Your Child

Even warm days can begin as cool mornings or give way to chilly evenings, so it is essential that your child be properly dressed.

The key is to clothe him in layers that effectively trap his body heat and allow you to remove and replace particular garments as necessary. In cold weather, start with warm underwear, such as a polypropylene shirt and shorts. In extreme conditions, you can put regular underwear over the polypropylene, although a turtleneck shirt, pants, sweater, and wool socks may be sufficient. Outerwear, such as a down vest and a heavy jacket or parka, should be wind- and water-resistant.

A baby immobilized in a carrier should be dressed in layers topped with a warm bunting bag or a down- or polyester-filled baby snowsuit. Overmittens, as well as mittens, are a must; so is a hat, since a substantial portion of body heat is lost through the head and neck. An older child may prefer a balaclava, a wool cap that can be rolled down to protect the ears, face, and neck.

No matter how balmy the day, you should bring a jacket or sweater for your youngster to wear. Cotton fabrics provide protection from the sun while allowing adequate ventilation, but polyester fabrics are good for wet conditions. It is also wise to bring a lightweight poncho or rain suit consisting of pants and a jacket. A one-piece rain suit is suitable for small infants and toddlers. A rain cap or hooded jacket will keep his head dry.

Good footwear is just as important as good clothing. For rough terrain, lightweight hiking boots are a good investment, although high-top sneakers will do. (Be sure to break the boots in beforehand.) Wet weather calls for waterproof boots of a leather-rubber construction. Attachable nylon gaiters keep snow and gravel out of the shoes.

Bunting bag

One-piece rain suit

Hiking boots

Waterproof boots

Gaiters

Jacket

Down vest

Polypropylene underwear

Rain jacket

Rain pants

Poncho

Balaclava

Rain cap

Overmittens

117

Hiking, Biking, and Cross-Country Skiing

For most families, it is a good idea to make an initial hike, bike trip, or cross-country ski trek a fairly short one over familiar ground. Such excursions, which might last from half an hour to all day, require minimal planning and expertise but still hold the promise of wholesome family fun and shared adventure. And they are good indicators of whether more ambitious trips should be undertaken. When you are ready to go on longer expeditions, common sense dictates that two adults go along, rather than one, for safety reasons as well as the practical one of sharing any load.

Basic hiking equipment

If your excursions will lead to full-scale backpacking *(page 122)*, now might be the time to invest in hiking boots *(page 116)*; otherwise, sneakers or walking shoes will do fine. If you plan on spending a few hours outdoors, bring a daypack to hold a jacket or sweater, a snack, something to drink, sunscreen, a first-aid kit *(page 135)*, and any other odds and ends that you might need. A toddler or older preschooler may enjoy the importance of carrying her own child-size pack, even if it contains only a sandwich or carton of juice. If you have an infant or toddler in tow, you will need either a sling-type carrier or a back carrier *(page 115)*. An older child may still require a carrier, and bringing it will spare you the discomfort of having to piggyback a wriggling three- or four-year-old.

What to expect on the trail

Before you set out, realistically assess how far and how fast your little one can comfortably walk *(box, below)*. Remember, those short legs tire quickly. You do not want to turn what ought to

How Far Can Children Hike?

This chart shows how many minutes preschoolers of various ages can be expected to walk and the distances they might cover before needing a rest stop. On rugged terrain, the times and distances will be less. Children younger than three must be carried, although a sturdy toddler might be encouraged to walk for ten minutes. After a few outings with your child, you will have a good idea of her stamina. Praise of her efforts will help greatly in keeping her happily moving along.

Toddler   75 yards

3- to 5-year-old   ¼ mile

6-year-old   ½ mile

10-15 minutes

20-25 minutes

30-45 minutes

A mother and her son and daughter enjoy a late-afternoon hike along an arid backcountry trail. When hiking with young children, stop often for rest and snacks and allow plenty of exploring time.

be a pleasant outing into an unpleasant time for everyone.

With an infant, your hikes will be limited largely by your own stamina, since the baby will be riding on your back. Lulled by your rocking stride, he may even fall asleep in the carrier. An older baby, however, may grow restless, so you would be wise to bring some creative distractions. For starters, try tying soft toys to the baby carrier and keeping a small supply of finger foods in a convenient place.

Too heavy to carry for any great distance but not yet a strong walker, a toddler is another story. Alternating between walking and riding is the obvious solution, but not always easy to accomplish. A strong-willed two-year-old bent on asserting his independence may insist on walking; let him try for a while—he is bound to see sooner or later that it is much nicer to be carried. Be prepared for him to insist also on pausing to investigate every rock and fallen log. Your best approach to this behavior is simply to relax and let him proceed at his own pace. After all, what is the rush? If, for some reason, you really must keep moving, try striking a deal with him; promise a snack or cool drink when he reaches a certain point farther up the trail. Even an older preschooler may need frequent rest stops and perhaps some stories or songs along the way to keep his mind occupied as he walks.

Planning a bicycle outing

For families with young children, bicycling can be a delightful alternative to hiking. You may eventually need a good ten-speed or all-terrain bicycle if you ride on unpaved roads or paths. But at first, for short distances over flat ground, any bike in decent condition will do fine. An infant can ride on your back in a carrier, while an older baby or toddler can travel in a child's bicycle seat attached over the rear wheel *(below)*. You can let your five- or six-year-old bring her own bike if she can both ride along the side of the road without wavering from side to side and, when turning, give hand signals without losing her balance. Don't expect her to keep up with your speed, however; you will have to slow down for her benefit.

When buying a child's seat, choose a model that provides good back and side support. The assembly should include a strong safety belt and a plastic foot guard to prevent little feet from accidentally swinging into the spokes. Everyone should wear a crash helmet, especially if you are cycling in traffic. (You will not, of course, want any child cycling where there is traffic.) A small rearview mirror that clips onto a helmet or pair of glasses is a valuable accessory. The mirror allows you to keep track of automobile traffic without constantly turning your head and risking loss of balance. A horn or bell to warn pedestrians or other bikers is another good safety device. And remember to maintain a safe speed going downhill, and to be alert for patches of sand or gravel that could cause you to skid and possibly spill.

Dogs, even friendly ones, can be a hazard for the bicyclist. If a dog suddenly darts into your path when you are riding, dismount and walk the bicycle, keeping it between you and the dog; do not attempt to outrace the animal. Once the dog recognizes you as a human being, almost always, it will quickly lose interest.

Introducing cross-country skiing

Cross-country skiing with an infant on your back is only slightly more difficult than skiing unencumbered, but you may find

Safety is a top priority for cyclist and passenger alike. This mother and child are both wearing crash helmets, and the child is securely belted in a high-backed bucket seat that will provide protection in the event of a mishap.

it impossible with a restless two-year-old. Nonetheless, by the time your child is three or four years old, he can probably begin learning himself. Lessons may best be left until your child is a little older. For the time being, your little one will probably learn just as quickly by following your lead. Try showing him how in your backyard. When he is ready for the first family outing, limit his efforts to about half an hour. A five- or six-year-old may be able to chug along for a longer period of time, assuming you stop occasionally for rest and an energy-boosting snack.

Wait until the sun has had time to warm the air a little before venturing out, and do not stay out after sundown when the air has become frigid. Remember, children lose body heat much more rapidly than adults do, and you certainly do not want to let your child get chilled *(pages 134-135)*. The best way to keep him warm is to dress him in a wool hat and several layers of wool or synthetic-fill clothing. Bring at least one pair of extra mittens. If your child gets warm enough that sweat starts soaking the inner layers of his clothing, remove an outer layer, but be sure to replace it during rest stops. An infant on your back is not generating the additional heat that you are as you ski, so do take special care to bundle him well in several layers of clothing under his snowsuit.

Cross-country ski equipment Children's cross-country ski equipment, especially the boots, can be expensive. You may want to try skiing with secondhand equipment, which you may be able to purchase at a yard sale or local ski swap. Waxless skis, rather than skis with waxable bottoms, are the easiest for children to use. Their molded bottoms are suitable for all snow conditions.

When you are selecting skis for your child, bear in mind the general rule that cross-country skis, stood on end, should reach between head-high and wrist-high when your youngster's arm is extended overhead. Buy skis for next year, and with luck you will get three years' use. Rather than pin-type ski bindings, look for adjustable ones, which do not call for special boots. Your child can then wear regular hiking boots *(page 116)* or rubber boots with sturdy soles over insulated booties or woolen socks. If you do invest in cross-country ski boots, pick ones that are roomy enough for your child to wear two pairs of heavy socks and one pair of thin ones; next winter, after her feet have grown, you can eliminate one pair of heavy socks and still have boots that fit. Ski poles, too, are not necessary for beginners. Unless they are included in a ski package, put off buying them until your youngster is older. ❖

Some Practical Advice

If you and your youngster have enjoyed your day trips together, you may now want to try overnight camping with her. But before heading for the outback, consider carefully the style of camping that is most suitable for your family. There is no need to feel compelled to rough it. You can be close to nature simply by renting a cabin in a wilderness area or national park. Camping from a car or recreational vehicle is another possibility. (See page 139 for information about renting RVs.) For some families, however, camping, by definition, means sleeping under the stars or in a tent and cooking meals over a portable stove or open fire. And for the truly hardy, there is only one way—backpacking.

Backpacking with children

As its name implies, backpacking involves toting all your food and equipment with you. If your child is neither old enough to walk several miles on his own nor young enough to be carried on your back while your spouse or another adult carries the gear, you may want to postpone this activity for a few years. A three- or four-year-old can use a daypack, while a sturdy six-year-old may be able to handle a framepack *(page 115)*. Keep your child's load small. On subsequent trips, you can gradually increase the weight. And just as you did on your day hikes, do not plan to cover too much ground at a time. Praise his accomplishments, however small, and stop often. When you do, be sure to give him a chance to sail twigs down a stream, skip pebbles across a pond, or chat with the ranger at a fire tower.

A young camper zips up the family tent to keep out marauding animals. Assisting with simple camping chores can give a youngster a sense of responsibility and accomplishment.

Woodsy Owl says
GIVE A HOOT!
DON'T POLLUTE!

Setting up camp

Whether you trek in or drive in, look for a level site on which to pitch your tent and set up camp, preferably on ground that is high enough to avoid flooding in a heavy rain, and close to a source of water. (See page 125 for drinking precautions.) Do not make camp close to cliffs, lakeshores, rivers, poison ivy, or other obvious hazards.

Take a few minutes to spell out precisely the limits beyond which your child must not venture by herself. To make sure that she stays in sight while you are setting up camp for the night, encourage her to lend you a hand with the tent and sleeping bags. Some parents find it helpful to give their child a whistle to blow should she accidentally stray from the campsite and become lost. You might want to tell her that in the unlikely event you and she become separated, she should stay right where she is until you come to find her; she should not try to make her way back to you on her own.

Toilet facilities

Unless you are camping in an established area with outhouses or bathrooms, you should give immediate attention to setting up a toilet area. Pick a location 200 to 300 feet from your campsite, far from any water source and at a spot where no one else is ever likely to camp. Accompany your youngster to the toilet area so that she cannot wander off. To dispose of wastes, use the "cat-hole" method: Using either a camp shovel or a trowel, dig a small hole no more than six inches deep. Once wastes and toilet tissue have been deposited, show your child how to cover the hole with a layer of dirt.

Disposable diapers are not biodegradable and must not be buried in the toilet area or elsewhere. As disagreeable as it might be, you will have to pack out the soiled ones. A better idea is to bring cloth diapers for your baby. You can wash them in a container and air-dry them. (Discard the water onto the ground, not into a stream, well away from the campsite.) A paper liner will make washing easier; you can simply bury the soiled liner in the toilet area.

How much food to bring

The duration of your stay in the wild and whether you are traveling by car or on foot will determine how much food you are able to bring. The fresh air is likely to produce big appetites, particularly if you are getting lots of exercise, so it is wise to bring more food than your family would normally eat. You should also be sure to include plenty of high-energy snacks. Beef jerky and dried fruit are especially good choices. One veteran parent-backpacker suggests carrying enough food for "at least an

---

The Dos and Don'ts of Camping

Teach your children to observe the motto of Woodsy Owl *(above)*, America's antipollution symbol, and then follow these sensible rules:
- Use stoves for cooking rather than building fires. (When you must build a fire, follow the precautions described on page 127.)
- Do not alter a campsite in any way. Leave it cleaner than you found it. This means removing all of your trash.
- Never throw your dishwater into a lake or stream.
- Dig latrine holes six inches deep, at least 200 to 300 feet from water sources. Refill the holes with the original sod.
- Leave pets at home. If pets are allowed, be sure to keep your animal on a leash.
- Preserve quiet.

adult, or even an adult and a half, for every child on the trip."

The proliferation of lightweight, easy-to-prepare dehydrated and freeze-dried foods, available in sporting-goods stores and some supermarkets, makes it possible to enjoy many of the same foods you eat at home. Besides such mainstays as stew, chili, and hot dogs, you can enjoy soups, spaghetti, omelets, potatoes, cheese, fruit, and meat. You can even treat your family to beef stroganoff, shrimp creole, beef burgundy, and other gourmet fare. Tasty freeze-dried desserts are also available.

Many meals can be made in a single pot simply by stirring the dried ingredients into boiling water and cooking them briefly. Some packaged foods let you dispense with the pot; you simply pour hot water into the foil package and stir.

Perishable foods If weight is no problem, you may choose to bring along perishable foods, packed in a cooler with plenty of ice. But do not expect the food to remain edible for much more than twenty-four hours unless it is wintertime and the weather is near freezing. During the drive to the campsite, the cooler and the foods that you have packed in it will stay cold for a longer period of time if you can store it in the passenger section of the car, rather than in the trunk.

When you reach your destination, set the cooler in the shade, wrapped in newspapers and covered by a sleeping bag to insulate it from the heat. These precautions are particularly important in hot weather. When the temperature is eighty degrees Farenheit and above, food bacteria multiply very rapidly, especially in fresh meat and poultry. Food poisoning is less of a threat in cooler weather, but bacteria can still flourish if the temperature is above sixty degrees for a long enough time. For that reason, if you plan to eat steaks or hamburgers as the first night's meal, pack the meat either frozen or partially frozen. Fresh fruits and vegetables are less likely to spoil rapidly, but they should be washed at home so you do not have to worry about purifying the water at the campsite. If you are bringing along bacon, lunch meat, or hot dogs for breakfast and lunch on the second day, you can be sure they are safe to eat if there are still chunks of ice floating in the water inside the cooler.

Feeding infants For the breast-feeding infant, life in the woods means little more than a change of scenery. But looking out for the nutritional needs of the bottle-fed infant is not so simple. Without refrigeration, milk spoils quickly, and canned formula is just as perishable once the tin has been opened. Your best bet is powdered

For Worry-Free Water

When camping, you will want to follow the rule of experienced campers: Never use untreated water for drinking or brushing teeth, no matter how inviting the source. Even an icy spring can harbor microscopic organisms that cause diarrhea, cramps, and more serious gastrointestinal afflictions, such as amoebic dysentery and giardiasis.

Many campers solve the problem by boiling their water. At sea level, five to ten minutes of boiling will kill even the hardiest waterborne pest. Add one minute of boiling time for each 1,000 feet of altitude. As the water cools, let any sediment settle and then pour off the purified water. You can improve the bland taste by pouring the water back and forth between containers to aerate it.

Another tried-and-true method is to treat the water with iodine. Two to four grams of iodine can be lethal if ingested, however, so keep kits containing iodine safely away from your children. And if you are pregnant or have a thyroid con-

dition, check with your doctor before using any iodine compound.

One practical kit consists of a one-ounce glass bottle containing several crystals of iodine. Fill the bottle with water and shake it vigorously, forming an iodine-water solution. Hold the bottle upright so that the undissolved crystals fall to the bottom. Follow the directions that accompany the kit, pouring an appropriate number of capfuls, based on the air temperature, into one liter (1.06 quarts) of water. (Be careful not to include any of the crystals.) Disinfection at seventy-seven degrees Fahrenheit, for example, is accomplished with five capfuls. Wait a half hour before drinking. The longer you let the water stand, the better it will taste.

Iodine is sold as a tincture, too. With a dropper, squeeze eight to ten drops of the tincture into one quart of water and wait thirty minutes. If the water is very cold, you may need to wait a full hour for purification to work. Should the water remain below sixty-eight degrees Fahrenheit, the solution may fail to kill the giardiasis parasites.

You can also buy iodine purification tablets. Add one tablet to a quart of water and set the liquid aside for at least thirty minutes. If the water is cloudy, resort to two tablets. They give the water a particularly strong iodine taste, but they are childproof. An entire fifty-tablet bottle contains only one-fiftieth of the lethal dose of iodine.

The high-tech method of purifying water is to use a filter device *(above)*. Most outfitters and camping-equipment stores stock several brands that fit nicely into a backpack and are simple to use. The pore holes should be less than two microns (two-millionths of a meter) wide to trap the tiniest germs and pests.

You may want to bring along some powdered soft-drink mixes to make the water more palatable.

---

formula—provided that your baby likes it and you have an available supply of pure water. Discard any not drunk, since formula keeps no better than any other milk product. Do the same with opened jars of baby food. Instant baby food to which you add hot water is easier to carry than the jars. But make sure your baby is used to eating it before your trip.

Storing food and garbage
Most parks warn campers to store food in a manner that will not attract wild animals. Bears are the most dangerous scavengers, but you also do not want a porcupine, raccoon, or skunk prowling your campsite. The best storage method is to put the food into a nylon sack and suspend it with a rope from a high tree branch about ten feet off the ground. Your local outfitter may sell a sack designed for this purpose. You must take the same precautions with your garbage, because it will be every bit as appetizing to a hungry animal as your food supply. Only established campsites have trash receptacles, so be sure to bring

plastic trash bags so that you will be able to carry out your leftovers when you break camp.

The well-equipped outdoor kitchen

A lightweight stove, fuel, a nesting set of stainless-steel pots and skillets, a few cooking utensils, and a plate, cup, fork, and spoon for each family member form the backbone of the outdoor kitchen. Other handy items include pliers for removing hot pots from the stove, a Swiss army knife as an all-purpose tool, and empty plastic film containers as dispensers of salt, pepper, spices, and herbs. If you are camping from a car, bring a cooler for storing perishables.

Be sure to include biodegradable detergent in your kit. After scrubbing each dish in boiled water, discard the dirty water 200 to 300 feet from any water source and boil another potful for rinsing. Dry the dishes with a towel or air-dry them in a mesh bag hung from a tree branch.

To build a campfire or not?

You may warmly remember your own childhood experiences around a campfire—stories, songs, marshmallows, the final dying embers before sleep. Like most parents, you probably wish to share these experiences with your own children. And at some campsites, including many national forests, you can do so; but laws prohibiting or restricting campfires depend on the site you visit and the time of year. Constant fire damage to forests and the stripping of woodland areas by campers have resulted in widespread restrictions on fires. To establish the right cozy atmosphere, a camp lantern, with its circle of light, can be a good substitute for a campfire.

Before building any fire, always check local and state regulations. You may need a license or permit, or there may be only certain sites where fires are permitted. Make sure you know how to build one and how to use it for cooking *(box, opposite).* Otherwise, bring a portable stove.

Kinds of stoves

Modern cooking stoves are lightweight, easy to use, and safe, the latter an important factor to consider when backpacking with children. There are three types, categorized by the fuel they burn: white gas, kerosene, and either butane or propane.

White-gas stoves are the choice of most backpackers. They are extremely light, usually weighing less than two pounds, and as their name implies, operate not on gasoline, but on white

Select a camping stove based on your mode of transportation. If weight is no concern, buy a large model that combines high fuel capacity with easy starting (below, right). For backpacking, use a lightweight model (below, left).

How to Build a Safe Campfire

If you must build a campfire, experts suggest that you always build the smallest fire necessary for your purposes. A small fire, such as the classic Indian-tepee fire described here, will burn down easily to ashes, and you can put it out quickly.

In constructing your fire, remember three safety precautions: First, never build a fire on a dry, windy day, since it can spread too easily. Second, never leave a fire unattended, even for a few minutes. Third, keep a bucket of water handy in case the fire does get out of control.

If possible, build your fire in an existing fire circle, since each new circle creates additional soil damage. If you must use unspoiled ground, choose an open space, well away from tents, equipment, tree roots, overhanging branches, or spongy soil. Avoid any situations in which sparks may smolder in the soil or fly into tree branches. Make sure the fire is at least 200 feet from a water source, to avoid pollution. Clear a ten-foot diameter *(below)*, heaping burnable materials outside the circle. Once you hit bare ground, you can begin.

Burn only organic matter, such as dead twigs and fallen branches; and avoid tree stumps or trunks, which house and

feed insect and animal life. Some campers like to place a semicircle of reflector rocks around the fire to contain it and shield it from the wind. If you do use rocks, avoid sandstone or shale, which can explode under high temperatures.

Children enjoy looking for tinder, searching the forest floor for dry pine needles and moss, fallen branches, twigs, and birch bark. Use deadwood only. Break up the branches into pieces, using your ax or hatchet to split the thicker ones.

When you have gathered an ample supply of wood, you are ready to begin. First, heap tinder in the center of your site *(above)*. Next, lean sticks around the tinder like tepee poles. When the tinder is surrounded by sticks, light it and gradually feed in thicker pieces of wood from the downwind side. To cook, simply place a folding grill over the fire.

Do not attempt to put out the fire until the coals have burned to ashes. Your child will probably enjoy sprinkling water on the ashes as you mix them into the soil with a stick. Rake through the dampened ashes again to expose any hot coals; sprinkle on more water if necessary. Last, bury the ashes and wet down the soil around the fire ring.

gas—a fuel readily available by the gallon can at hardware stores and outfitters. Lighting these stoves can be tricky, so practice at home before beginning your trip. Most of them must be preheated by igniting a small amount of fuel in the priming cup to build up vapor pressure in the fuel tank; only then will the valve that controls the gas open so that the stove can be lit. White-gas stoves also start sluggishly in cold weather, although some models are equipped with hand-operated fuel pumps that negate the need for priming and make them more suitable for winter use.

Kerosene stoves are the safest to operate because kerosene is less combustible than gas. They also work well in all weather. But kerosene stoves are messy; they are susceptible to smoking, generate soot, and emit a bothersome odor. Also, kerosene is not available as readily as white gas.

The third type, the cartridge stove, uses precharged canisters of butane or propane gas for its source of fuel. These stoves are the easiest to operate; simply insert a cartridge, open the valve, and apply a match. They do not generate as much heat as white-gas or kerosene stoves, however, so food takes longer to cook. As time goes by and the cartridge is depleted, the stoves give off less and less heat, but you cannot insert a new cartridge until the old one is completely empty.

Stove safety No matter what type of stove you use, never refuel it inside a tent or near an open flame, because there is danger of an ex-

plosion. All stoves generate deadly carbon monoxide; in the event of rain, cook under a tarp—not inside your tent—to permit adequate ventilation. If you run out of fuel, be sure to let the stove cool before refilling its tank. Store extra white gas or kerosene in special aluminum bottles or steel flasks, not in easily punctured plastic containers. Finally, be sure to keep stored fuel away from heat and out of direct sunlight.

Sleeping arrangements

Sleeping arrangements are a simple matter of laying out the sleeping bags in a manner that makes best use of available tent space. Some possible configurations are shown at right. As your child grows older, and especially if you have more than one youngster, you may find it more suitable to use two small tents for the family rather than one large one. Some adult bags can be zipped together to form the outdoor equivalent of a double bed, leaving enough room to tuck a small child in the middle. An older preschooler will need her own sleeping bag.

These configurations of sleeping bags in three different tents work well for a family of four. Most children love the snuggly closeness guaranteed by a small tent; it helps them feel secure—and it is fun.

There are many models of sleeping bags to choose from. Some manufacturers make down-filled foot sacks, half-size sleeping bags used by mountain climbers in conjunction with down-filled parkas, which can serve as sleeping bags for children up to six years of age.

Try to maintain the same bedtime schedule for your child that you have at home. If she is used to a midafternoon nap, by all means take a break and allow her to rest. Likewise, if she normally goes to bed at eight o'clock, make sure she has been happily tucked into her sleeping bag by that time.

Some children experience a heightened fear of darkness outdoors. Having you nearby will provide the surest comfort, but it may help if she has her favorite doll, stuffed animal, or blanket with her. Reassure her that her fears are imaginary, and if need be, keep a lighted lantern outside the tent until you are

Seated on a log outside their tent, father and son share a bedtime story by the glow of lantern light. Maintaining bedtime rituals can help a child sleep well in unfamiliar surroundings.

An Expert's View

ready to join her inside.

Lights out No camping trip would be complete without bringing the day to a close with a song or a story. A campfire *(page 127)* is a great mood-setter, but is certainly not a requirement. All that is really needed are a repertory of songs, a few favorite storybooks, and your own enthusiasm. You might even want to make a game of the storytelling by having one family member begin a story and the rest add to the tale as it makes the rounds. Ghost stories are, of course, a traditional part of camp life, but they are better postponed until your youngster is a little older and less likely to be frightened by them.

A camping trip is also a great time for stargazing. Away from the lights of populated areas, lying with your backs to the ground and your eyes to the sky, you can look for shooting stars or try to identify constellations *(page 38)*.

Breaking camp When the time comes to move on, be as careful in quitting your campsite as you were in choosing it. Allow plenty of time to stow your gear and strike the tent. Encourage your child to give you some help policing the area: making sure the campfire is completely doused, cleaning up any bits of trash, and filling in the holes left by tent stakes. Your goal should be to erase, as much as possible, any sign that you slept there and to leave the site in better condition than you found it. This is a lesson that will not be lost on your youngster. •:•

Traveling by Water

Traveling by canoe, kayak, rowboat, or other craft is a wonderful way for families with small children to penetrate remote areas. You can carry more gear than you can backpacking, and most youngsters adore being on the water. For many people, there is no more pleasurable pastime. But whereas every reasonably fit person can safely hike, boating requires expertise, especially on a river with a swift, tricky current or on a large lake, where a sudden change in the weather can turn still water choppy and menacing. Before you take your family canoe or kayak camping, make sure that you know your own limits and can exercise good judgment. Water-related accidents often happen when inexperienced people try to do too much. Bear in mind as well that most accidents occur when conditions seem perfect—in good weather, on small bodies of water—with the capsizing of a craft or someone falling overboard.

Basic boating equipment
If you plan to buy or rent a boat, first make sure that it suits your family's special needs. Most rowboats can accommodate two adults and a child and their gear, as can many canoes. A few double kayaks are suitable for one adult, a nonpaddling child, and their gear. Avoid any craft that requires tandem paddling if only you and your child are to be in it.

Provide each family member with a life jacket *(box, below)*, and include enough waterproof bags to stow equipment. Life jackets and bags can be purchased at water-sports stores. You

A Lifesaver for Children

Children around water, especially those who cannot swim, need protection as well as parental vigilance. One easy solution is to wear a life jacket, a vestlike piece of equipment that will keep your child afloat in the water.

Federal law requires all recreational boats to carry a Coast Guard-approved life jacket—a personal flotation device, or PFD—for each person aboard. Common sense also dictates that a PFD should be worn by every child and nonswimmer who is active near and certainly on water.

Which PFD you ought to buy depends on your child's size. In the Coast Guard classification system, a Type II PFD *(right)* is suitable for infants and children weighing less than fifty pounds. These life jackets are reasonably comfortable to wear and have the extra protection of a flotation collar that will hold the child's head above the water, even when she is unconscious. If your youngster weighs between fifty and ninety

pounds, buy a Type I PFD, which also is designed to keep the face in a safe, upright position.

Before you purchase any life jacket, check the label to make sure it has Coast Guard approval and have your child try it on for fit. Fasten the straps for her, grasp the jacket by the shoulders, and lift; if her chin and ears stay above the collar, the life jacket has the right degree of snugness.

Once your youngster has her own PFD, teach her to put it on by herself. Leave nothing to chance, however: Always check to make sure she has fastened the straps securely. Give her some time to practice floating in shallow water with the jacket on so that she knows how the jacket feels when it is doing its job. The PFD will not hold her head far above the water, but it will not let her sink and will keep her face in the air so that she can breathe; show her how to relax and let her legs dangle, and assure her that in an emergency situation, rescue would be quickly on its way.

Before storing your family's PFDs, air-

dry them thoroughly. Never put them on a radiator or other direct heat source; the heat can damage the flotation material. Inspect the PFDs before each outing to make sure they are still good; if a jacket is punctured or mildewed, buy a new one. Your child's life can depend on it.

may also want to bring floating cushions and kneepads, which add comfort to long trips. Be sure to wear clothing appropriate to the season and to pack rainwear. Avoid a rain poncho, however; it can envelop a person in the water and cause drowning.

Gliding in a canoe along the shoreline of a far-north lake, a mother and son watch a caribou stride through the shallows. Water travel gives access to many otherwise unreachable wilderness areas.

Teaching your child water safety

Rowboats virtually never tip over, and if you use common sense, there is little likelihood your canoe or kayak will capsize. But you will want to be prepared for all eventualities, and learning about boating safety can be great fun for your child—as well as a powerful incentive to learn how to swim. Check to find out if your local Red Cross chapter gives safety classes and children's swimming lessons.

Begin by teaching your youngster the various parts of the craft. Explain the proper way to get in and out and how to sit and move without upsetting the boat. Once she has absorbed these basics, strap her into a life jacket and move into shallow water. You too should put on a life jacket. Your example will emphasize to your child far better than words the necessity of wearing this important safety device.

Next, explain the importance of always staying with the craft. A capsized canoe or kayak is virtually unsinkable and makes a perfect life raft. Teach your youngster what to do should she accidentally fall in. Help her gently into the water, encouraging her to relax and making sure she holds onto the side of the craft.

Then let her practice climbing back in or on top. Repeat the exercise, gradually moving into deeper water, until you both feel confident.

The next step is to stage a capsizing while you and your child are in the vessel. Tip over the craft, right it, and retrieve the paddles. Then the two of you can climb back inside and bail out the swamped vessel by scooping the water out with your hands or a plastic bucket—an activity in which your child will probably join enthusiastically. As before, go through the drill several times, until you are sure that she is at ease floating in her life jacket in water well over her head.

If she is an older preschooler, as part of her safety lessons, you may also want to show her the rudiments of paddling or rowing, although you should not expect a five- or six-year-old to paddle or row effectively.

Starting out

Short day trips in calm, protected water are the sensible way to get your family's feet wet. After several such outings, you may feel ready to try an overnight camping trip.

Plan your itinerary carefully. Get a map and chart your course, estimating travel times from point to point. Allow extra time so that you can stay ashore on windy days, when the water is rough and paddling will be too exhausting. Make sure you build in plenty of rest stops, too. A half-hour pause in a shallow cove for some swimming, wading, or exploring is an ideal way to vent youthful energy. Be prepared with songs and games; they will make a canoe trip more fun.

Before you start out on a trip, study the water you will be traveling over. Obviously, you will want to avoid rivers with stretches of white water or waterways that require portages. Even so, it is a wise precaution to follow the example of many canoe campers and lash your equipment to the craft by wrapping a length of rope around the center thwart, or crosspiece, and lacing it through each piece of gear.

Introducing your child to fishing

If you plan well, your unhurried travel by water should leave time for fishing. There is hardly a child who will not leap at the chance to try his luck. But be sure to check the local fishing regulations before you go. You may have to get a fishing license, and there may be rules governing the sizes and kinds of fish you are allowed to catch.

Few sports are so respectful of a beginner's lack of exper-

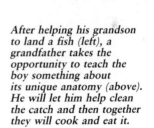

tise. A three- or four-year-old can happily pass the time with a safety pin attached to a length of line, while an older youngster can be outfitted with a real rod and hook. When no one is using it, embed the barb in a piece of cork to prevent it from snagging you or your child.

Be vigilant while your child is fishing. In a tippy canoe, or even in a rowboat, a sudden movement could be enough to topple him into the water. Fishing from a pier puts him on firmer ground but also raises the possibility of his accidentally tumbling in. You may feel more comfortable having him wear a life jacket, just as in a boat.

Worms are the most popular fishing bait, and they are fun to dig up. If you do not have access to a garden, you can also buy them cheaply from a bait shop. To bait the hook, slip it into one end of the worm, embedding and concealing the point. Now show your child how to drop his line over the edge of the pier or the gunwale of the boat. Demonstrate for him how to pull up sharply on the rod to snag the hook in the fish's mouth should he get a bite. Youthful attention spans being short, he may need a few gentle reminders that fish do not always cooperate and that fishing takes patience.

Make sure that you have been fishing in unpolluted waters before you make the decision to keep your catch. And if you are going to throw a fish back, always wet your hands before pulling out the hook. That way, you will not remove the slime that coats the fish's body and protects it from disease. And whether you are keeping the fish or not, do not entrust the task of removing the hook to your child. Fish often swallow the hook, making extraction quite difficult, and many fish have thorny fins that give nasty pricks. Tell your youngster that he will be able to do it for himself when he is a little older. After you have unhooked the fish, give your child a chance to examine it; take the opportunity to point out the gills, fins, and scales that make fish unique. Catching his first fish will be a special event, one that your child will probably never forget. ❖

After helping his grandson to land a fish (left), a grandfather takes the opportunity to teach the boy something about its unique anatomy (above). He will let him help clean the catch and then together they will cook and eat it.

Ensuring a Safer Camping Trip

The Boy Scout motto Be Prepared is a good one to keep in mind when you camp. You are unlikely to encounter a life-threatening emergency, but it makes sense to be ready.

First-aid training

Although it is by no means a prerequisite for short trips, taking a basic first-aid class that includes instruction in cardiopulmonary resuscitation (CPR) is recommended by many outdoor specialists. Hospitals, local wilderness groups, and the Red Cross offer such instruction at low cost.

Simply going through first-aid training will make you more safety-conscious, more aware of the causes of accidents and how they can be prevented. Also, your newfound confidence in your ability will increase your family's sense of security. Equally important, you will be teaching your child a valuable lesson—the importance of developing personal responsibility for others. When she gets older, she will probably want to learn the lifesaving skills herself.

Snakebites

There are, of course, real dangers in the wilderness (pages 136-138), and one that looms large in many people's imagination is snakebite. The fact is that snakes pose little danger to campers in the United States. The vast majority are not venomous, and those that are would rather flee than attack a human being. Snakes strike only when they perceive a threat to their safety. Thus, the chances that your youngster or anyone else in your party will be bitten are very small indeed. What is more likely to happen is that you may come across a nonvenomous snake sunning itself on some rocks. No doubt your little one will be thrilled, provided you treat the event for what it is, a priceless opportunity to observe an animal in its wild state.

Most experts recommend that, in the unlikely event that a member of the family is bitten by a poisonous snake, you wash the wound well and keep the victim as calm as possible. The bitten limb should be immobilized and the victim placed in a position so that the wound is lower than the heart, to slow the action of the venom through the system. Do not try to treat the victim yourself by making an incision over the fang marks and attempting to suck out the venom, a technique you may have seen heroes in old movies employ. In fact, by doing so you would probably extract only an insignificant amount of venom at best, and would certainly risk creating an infection—to say nothing of the possibility of cutting nerves and ligaments. Instead, apply a tourniquet above the bite. But bear in mind that this is a tricky procedure. The tourniquet must be tight enough to stop the spread of the venom, but not so tight as to cut off the blood supply to the affected part.

Carry the victim out, and in situations permitting it, send your spouse or another adult ahead to call for medical help. Do not stop to find the snake, but if you do happen to kill it, bring it along so that a positive identification can be made and the proper antivenom serum applied swiftly.

Venomous spider bites and insect stings

Unlike snake bites, spider bites and bee stings are a common occurence on camping trips. In the vast majority of instances, the bites are only annoying. But some children are highly allergic to the venom; the resulting condition, known as anaphylactic shock, can be life-threatening. If you think that your child is likely to have such a reaction, consult your family doctor before you go into the wilds. The physician can give you a prescription for preventive medicine; some doctors recommend that parents take along an antivenom kit just in case. In the eventuality you have no kit with you, administer CPR and elevate the victim's feet—and get her to a doctor or hospital as soon as possible.

To guard against spider and insect bites, you should inspect your child's bedding before she gets in at night and turn her boots or sneakers upside down and shake them out before she puts them on in the morning.

Of course, you will try not to camp in areas heavily infested with mosquitoes, black flies, sand flies, ticks, no-see-ums, or biting gnats. But if you do, wear protective clothing, covering your head and neck with a hat or scarf, and apply insect repellent. Most experts recommend a repellent composed of at least 12 percent DEET, the acronym for the chemical diethyltoluamide. With children younger than two, apply DEET to the skin only once in any twenty-four-hour period; it may be applied to their clothing more often, and it will be just as effective. Do not let older children apply it to themselves; do it for them. Insect repellent, which is poisonous if ingested, must be used judiciously; it should be kept out of the eyes, and in heavy concentration can cause skin irritation. Remember too that water will wash it off, so if you go swimming or bathe, reapply the repellent after you are dry.

Preventing thermal injury

Small children adjust more slowly than adults to extreme weather conditions and are thus more susceptible to wide swings in body temperature. This is why it is so important to carry extra jackets and sweaters to put on your youngster under chilly conditions and to have her wear layers of clothing that can be taken off when she begins to sweat (page 116).

Any rapid loss of body heat—from exposure to cold weather, freezing rain, a dunking in cold water, or even excessive sweating followed by a sudden chill—can dangerously lower body temperature, creating a condition known as hypothermia. Watch your child to make sure she stays warm and dry. At the first sign of shivering, warm her up by adding another sweater or sweatshirt. If she shows difficulty talking and moving, wrap her in a reflective space blanket *(page 112)* or crawl into your sleeping bag, put her in it beside you, and hug her. The direct contact with your body heat should warm her sufficiently.

In cold weather, parents need also to watch for signs of frostbite—the freezing of skin tissue indicated by red or waxy-looking skin. Make sure your youngster wears mittens, but if you suspect superficial frostbite of her fingers, have her warm her hands by withdrawing them into her jacket through her sleeves. (This avoids having to open the jacket and release warmth.) You can warm her feet by cupping them in your hands inside a space blanket or sleeping bag.

On a hot day, overheating—a measurable elevation in body temperature—can result in heat exhaustion or dehydration. You can easily prevent this by maintaining a relaxed pace in your activities and providing your child with plenty of fluids.

If your child suffers a thermal injury of any kind, including a bad sunburn, check with your pediatrician as soon as you can.

General safety tips

Prevention is a word always to keep in mind when it comes to the wilderness. Experience has taught that it pays to heed the following suggestions:

Before you begin a backcountry hike or a canoe trip, provide a forest ranger or other park official with your itinerary, including your expected time and place of arrival. This way, authorities will know where to look for you if you get lost.

If you are going on a day hike at a state park, leave a note on the dashboard of your car. Print it in large letters, indicating the name of the trail you are taking and the date and time you expect to return. Rangers patrol the parking lots, and they will take notice if you do not return for your car.

To keep children from straying, one adult should walk at the front of your party and another bring up the rear.

If you are caught out in a thunderstorm, stay away from single trees or large boulders, because lightning is attracted to isolated objects. Avoid hilltops and ridges. If you are swimming or boating, proceed to shore immediately. Seek shelter in a ravine or grove of low trees or bushes. If you are caught in an open area, lie flat on the ground until the storm passes.

As a preventive measure against rabies, tell your youngster not to get too close to wild animals you come across. Any mammal can carry rabies, but the disease is especially prevalent among foxes, raccoons, bats, and skunks.

A Family First-Aid Kit

Every family going on an outing should bring a first-aid kit for treating minor medical problems, such as cuts, scrapes, splinters, blisters, minor sprains, and sunburn. Many local chapters of the Red Cross, as well as outdoor-equipment stores, sell fully stocked kits. If you prefer, you can assemble your own, tailoring it to fit the specific needs of your family.

The alphabetical list here is for a family of four; it will help you decide what supplies to include in your kit. Be sure to pack child-strength medicines, in chewable tablets or liquid form. For carrying your supplies, choose a compact, lightweight bag or "organizer" with zippered or snap-on compartments. Check with your family doctor about the need for including prescription and allergy medicines and antivenom serum.

- acetaminophen (one adult-strength and one child-strength package), for pain and fever
- adhesive bandage strips, assorted sizes (one package), for small cuts
- adhesive tape (one-inch roll), for bandaging
- aerosol waterless cleanser (one can), for dressing wounds when water is not available
- alcohol swabs (one packet), for cleaning cuts
- antacid (24 tablets), for stomach upset and diarrhea
- antibacterial soap, for cleansing wounds
- antibiotic ointment, to prevent infections
- aspirin (one package), for adult minor headaches
- butterfly bandages (4 to 6), for closing wide cuts
- calamine lotion, for poison ivy and insect bites
- cotton balls (one package), for cleansing cuts and applying medication
- cotton-tip applicators (one package), for applying ointment
- elastic bandages, 4 inches wide (2), to wrap sprains or to use as slings
- first-aid manual
- gauze pads, 4 by 4 inches (10), to cover scrapes
- gauze pads, 5 by 9 inches, (4), to stanch bleeding
- manicure scissors, for cutting gauze and tape
- moleskin (4 sheets), for blisters
- safety pins (8), for fastening slings
- sewing needles (one package), for removing splinters
- sunscreen (one container), to prevent sunburn
- tweezers, for pulling splinters
- zinc oxide (one tube), for sunburn and skin irritation

Dangers of the Wild: Symptoms and Remedies

The chart that follows lists some of the poisonous wild plants and venomous insects and animals of the forty-eight contiguous states and gives symptoms and treatments. Check the maps for your area; study the specimens shown and avoid them. Be aware, however, that this is not a complete guide, especially for snakebites. Before going camping, provide yourself with medical training, such as CPR, and with first-aid manuals and supplies for areas where you will be.

Hazard	Habitat	Symptoms	Treatment
Poison ivy		Red skin, often with blisters; itching or burning; headache; fever	Remove and launder any clothing that has been contaminated. As soon as possible after contact, use soap and water to thoroughly wash any parts of the skin that may have touched the plant. Then swab affected areas freely with cotton balls, cloth, or tissues soaked in rubbing alcohol. To help relieve itching and burning, paint the rash generously with calamine lotion. Be alert for possible signs of shock or breathing difficulty if rash is severe or is on the face or genitals. If severe discomfort persists, seek medical assistance. *Prevention:* Dress yourself and your children in long-sleeved shirts and long pants or knee-high socks. Know how to recognize the plants, and stay away from them.
Pacific poison oak **Poison oak**		Same as for poison ivy, above	
Poison sumac		Same as for poison ivy, above	
Coral snake; harlequin, bead snake		Minor pain and swelling where bite occurred; blurred vision; droopy eyelids; drowsiness; drooling; nausea; sweating; difficulty breathing and speaking; possible shock and paralysis	Have person lie still, with bitten part lower than heart. Apply tourniquet—a belt, cloth strip, or elastic bandage will do—to bitten limb 2 to 4 inches above bite, or farther up, to avoid joint. This prevents venom from circulating. Be careful tourniquet is not too tight; adjust, if necessary, so your finger fits under it, blood oozes from bite, and pulse is felt farther out on limb. Check regularly, loosen further if necessary, but do not remove. If swelling reaches tourniquet, indicating spread of venom, apply another, 2 to 4 inches higher up, then remove the first. Wash bitten area thoroughly with soap and water to avoid infection. If you suspect coral-snake bite, flush wound repeatedly. Rattlesnake, copperhead bite: Follow procedures above. Be ready to treat for shock by administering CPR. Get medical help as soon as possible. Phone ahead to hospital, identifying type of snake.
Rattlesnake		Severe pain, with swelling of bitten area, discoloration of skin; general weakness; fast pulse; nausea; blurred vision; difficulty breathing; possible shock and convulsions	
Copperhead, adder, chunkhead, highland moccasin, pilot snake		Same as for rattlesnake, above	

Cottonmouth, water moccasin, water pilot snake  		*Same as for rattlesnake, opposite*	*Same as for rattlesnake, opposite*
Black widow spider  		*Immediate redness and sharp pain; sweating; nausea; stomach and muscle cramps; difficulty breathing; possible convulsions*	*Have victim lie still, with bitten part lower than heart. Apply a cold compress or ice wrapped in cloth; do not put ice directly on the skin. Be alert for any signs of shock or difficulty breathing. If necessary, administer CPR. Seek medical attention as quickly as possible. Prevention: Carry a walking stick to clear away webs across your path. Before picking up a branch or rock, roll it over first with your stick or your boot. Carry an insect spray designed to kill spiders, and use it when necessary on areas of deadwood or rocks near your campsite where you have reason to think spiders may be hiding. Always shake out sleeping bags and clothing before letting your family get into them, to clear them of any lurking spiders or insects.*
Brown recluse, violin spider 		*Delayed pain, 2 to 8 hours after bite; sweating; nausea; stomach and muscle cramps; difficulty breathing; possible convulsions*	
Tarantula  		*Usually only slight local pain; occasionally brings on reactions similar to bite by black widow spider (above) or leads to ulcer at site of bite*	
Bee; also wasp, hornet, killer bee, yellow jacket 		*Local swelling, pain, redness, itching, burning. Multiple stings may bring on headache, fever, muscle cramps; drowsiness, unconsciousness. Allergic reaction: facial swelling; weakness; wheezing; coughing; cramps, nausea; dizziness; blue skin; unconsciousness*	*Remove any stinger, without squeezing it. Wash all stings; apply calamine lotion. For allergic reaction, use antivenom kit prescribed by doctor or be prepared to treat for shock by administering CPR.*
Scorpion 		*Hot pain, tingling, or numbness; nausea, stomach cramps; fever; difficulty speaking; possible shock and convulsions*	*Same as for black widow spider, above. Prevention: Where scorpions are common, always shake out clothing and bedding before using. When lifting rocks and boards, lift with stick and beware of scorpions hiding underneath.*
Tick 		*Usually none; local infection if removal incomplete; possible later signs of serious diseases: Rocky Mountain spotted fever (fever, muscle aches, then spreading rash) and Lyme disease (circular lesions near bite, lethargy, joint and muscle pain)*	*Remove tick with tweezers. Wash bite thoroughly, and get medical help if it becomes infected, or for any fever in next 10 days. Prevention: Tuck pant legs into socks, spray with insect repellent. Check body daily.*

Chigger

Local burning or stinging; redness, swelling, and itching

Wash bites thoroughly; relieve itching with cold compresses or calamine lotion. Get medical help if scratching leads to infection, or for any fever within 10 days of insect bite. Prevention: Wear long pants, put insect repellent on boots and pant legs.

Fire ant

Blisters followed by intense itching

Apply cold compresses and administer pain medication. Seek medical attention. Prevention: Examine campsite for anthills and do not sleep near them.

Cone shell

Swelling, accompanied by pain, tingling, or numbness; dizziness, blurred vision; difficulty swallowing and breathing; possible collapse and paralysis

Same as for coral-snake bite, page 136. Soak wound in hot water for 30 minutes, then remove tourniquet. Watch for signs of shock or difficulty breathing. Get medical help.

Portuguese man-of-war, jellyfish

Burning pain; skin redness and rash; muscle cramps; nausea; possible difficulty breathing; possible shock

With hand wrapped in towel, wipe away all tentacles. Wash area with alcohol or ammonia diluted with saltwater (not fresh water). Watch carefully for signs of shock or breathing difficulty. Get medical attention.

Sea anemone, hydra

Burning pain; chills; stomach cramps, diarrhea

Soak the stung area in hottest water possible without scalding the victim. Seek medical attention, continuing hot soaks for 30 to 60 minutes while en route to doctor.

Stinging coral

Cuts, scrapes, bleeding, accompanied by burning pain

Wash wound thoroughly with soap and water. Watch carefully for signs of shock or difficulty breathing. Seek medical attention. Prevention: Wear canvas shoes or, if diving is planned, a rubber wet suit. For shell and coral collecting, wear heavy gloves.

Stingray

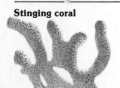

Lacerations or puncture wounds, with severe pain; pallor, then redness at wound; sweating, dizziness, nausea, weakness; possible paralysis and collapse

Remove visible fragments of stinger from in and around wound. Apply hot soaks for 30 to 60 minutes. Treat for shock and seek medical help. Watch breathing; be ready to give artificial respiration. Prevention: Slide feet, do not step, on seafloor.

Increasing Your Nature Knowledge

Wilderness and Nature Conservation Organizations

American Camping Association, Inc.
5000 State Road, 67 North
Martinsville, IN 46151

American Hiking Society
1015 31st Street NW
Washington, DC 20009

Appalachian Mountain Club
5 Joy Street
Boston, MA 02108

Appalachian Trail Conference
P.O. Box 807
Harpers Ferry, WV 25425

The Izaak Walton League of America, Inc.
1701 North Fort Myer Drive, Suite 1100
Arlington, VA 22209

National Audubon Society
950 Third Avenue
New York, NY 10022

National Park Service
Department of the Interior
Washington, DC 20240

National Wildlife Federation
1412 16th Street NW
Washington, DC 20036

Recreational Vehicle Rental Association
3251 Old Lee Highway, Suite 500
Fairfax, VA 22030

Sierra Club
730 Polk Street
San Francisco, CA 94109

The Sierra Club Foundation
730 Polk Street
San Francisco, CA 94109

United States Fish and Wildlife Service
Department of the Interior
Washington, DC 20240

United States Forest Service
Department of Agriculture
P.O. Box 2417
Washington, DC 20013

Map Distribution
United States Geological Survey
Box 25286 Federal Center
Denver, CO 80225

United States Nature Centers Directory
Natural Science for Youth Foundation
130 Azalea Drive
Roswell, GA 30075

The Wilderness Society
1400 I Street NW
Washington, DC 20005

Selected Books for Further Reading

CAMPING GUIDES

Backpacking with Babies and Small Children, by Goldie Silverman. Wilderness Press, 1986.

The Eddie Bauer Guide to Family Camping, by Archie Satterfield and Eddie Bauer. Addison-Wesley, 1982.

Introducing Your Kids to the Outdoors, by Joan Dorsey. Stone Wall Press, 1982.

Official Boy Scout Handbook, by William Hillcourt. Boy Scouts of America, 1986.

Starting Small in the Wilderness: The Sierra Club Outdoors Guide for Families, by Marlyn Doan. Sierra Club Books, 1979.

Take 'Em Along: Sharing the Wilderness with Your Children, by Barbara J. Euser. Cordillera, 1987.

ACTIVITY BOOKS

The Curious Naturalist, by John Mitchell. Prentice-Hall, 1980.

Do Animals Dream? Children's Questions about Animals Most Often Asked of the Natural History Museum, by Joyce Pope, Viking Press, 1986.

Hands-On Nature: Information and Activities for Exploring the Environment with Children, edited by Jenepher R. Lingelbach. Vermont Institute of Natural Science, 1987.

Hug a Tree: And Other Things to Do with Young Children, by Robert E. Rockwell et al. Gryphon House, 1985.

Mudpies to Magnets: A Preschool Science Curriculum, by Robert A. Williams et al. Gryphon House, 1987.

Sharing Nature with Children, by Joseph Bharat Cornell. Dawns Publications, 1979.

FIELD GUIDES

Audubon Society Pocket Guides. Beginner guides on birds, trees, wildflowers, etc. Knopf.

Golden Guides. A series of field guides on birds, trees, wildflowers, fossils, insects, reptiles, etc. Western Publishing.

Peterson's First Guides, by Roger Tory Peterson. A series of beginner field guides on birds, wildflowers, mammals, etc. Houghton Mifflin.

Stokes Nature Guides, by Donald W. Stokes and Lillian Q. Stokes. A series of field guides on animal and bird behavior. Little, Brown.

Tom Brown's Field Guides, by Tom Brown, Jr. A series on edible plants, animal tracking, nature observation, etc. Berkeley Publishing.

Bibliography

BOOKS

Allison, Linda, *The Reasons for Seasons: The Great Cosmic Megagalactic Trip without Moving from Your Chair*. Boston: Little, Brown, 1975.

Andry, Andrew C., and Steven Schepp, *How Babies Are Made*. Johannesburg, South Africa: Purnell, 1968.

Auerback, Paul S., M.D., *Medicine for the Outdoors: A Guide to Emergency Medical Procedures and First Aid*. Boston: Little, Brown, 1988.

Berrill, N. J., and Jacquelyn Berrill, *1001 Questions Answered about the Seashore*. New York: Dover, 1957.

Bonhivert, Edith, and Ernest Bonhivert, *Questions Children Ask*. Chicago: Standard Educational Corp., 1981.

Bramwell, Martyn, *Nature Study*. London: Piper, 1985.

Brown, Vinson, *Investigating Nature through Outdoor Projects: 36 Strategies for Turning the Natural Environment into Your Own Laboratory*. Harrisburg, Pa.: Stackpole, 1983.

Busch, Phyllis S., *Living Things That Poison, Itch, and Sting*. New York: Walker, 1976.

Calderone, Mary S., M.D., and Eric W. Johnson, *The Family Book about Sexuality*. New York: Harper and Row, 1981.

Caney, Steven, *Kids' America*. New York: Workman, 1978.

Carmichael, Viola S., *Science Experiences for Young Children*. Palo Alto, Calif.: R & E Research Associates, 1982.

Chinery, Michael, *Enjoying Nature with Your Family*. New York: Crown, 1977.

Conservation Directory 1988. Washington, D.C.: National Wildlife Federation, 1988.

Cooper, Elizabeth K., *Science in Your Own Back Yard*. New York: Harcourt, Brace and World, 1958.

Cornell, Joseph Bharat, *Sharing Nature with Children*. California: Ananda, 1979.

Court, Judith, *Ponds and Streams*. London: Franklin Watts, 1985.

De Cloux, Tina, and Rosanne Werges, *Tina's Science Notebook*. Covina, Calif.: Symbiosis Books, 1985.

Doan, Marlyn, *Starting Small in the Wilderness: The Sierra Club Outdoors Guide for Families*. San Francisco: Sierra Club Books, 1979.

Dorsey, Joan, *Introducing Your Kids to the Outdoors*. Washington, D.C.: Stone Wall Press, 1982.

Durrell, Gerald, and Lee Durrell, *The Amateur Naturalist*. New York: Alfred A. Knopf, 1983.

Fiarotta, Phyllis, and Noel Fiarotta, *Sticks & Stones & Ice Cream Cones*. New York: Workman, 1973.

Fichter, George S., *Keeping Amphibians and Reptiles as Pets*. New York: Franklin Watts, 1979.

Flemming, Bonnie Mack, and Darlene Softley Hamilton, *Resources for Creative Teaching in Early Childhood Education*. New York: Harcourt Brace Jovanovich, 1977.

Forgey, William W., M.D., *Wilderness Medicine*. Merrillville, Ind.: ICS Books, 1987.

Green, Martin I., *A Sigh of Relief: The First-Aid Handbook for Childhood Emergencies*. New York: Bantam Books, 1984.

Helms, Christopher L., *The Sonoran Desert*. Las Vegas, Nev.: KC Publications, 1983.

Hill, Katherine E., *Exploring the Natural World with Young Children*. New York: Harcourt Brace Jovanovich, 1976.

Hillcourt, William, *Offical Boy Scout Handbook*. Irving, Tex.: Boy Scouts of America, 1986.

Holt, Bess-Gene, *Science with Young Children*. Washington, D.C.: National Association for the Education of Young Children, 1977.

Hussey, Lois J., and Catherine Pessino, *Collecting for the City Naturalist*. New York: Thomas Y. Crowell, 1975.

Jones, Sandy, *Good Things for Babies*. Boston: Houghton Mifflin, 1980.

Katz, Adrienne, *Naturewatch: Exploring Nature with Your Children*. Reading, Mass.: Addison-Wesley, 1986.

Kemsley, William, *Backpacking Equipment Buyer's Guide*. New York: Collier Books, 1977.

Kemsley, William, Jr., ed., *The Whole Hiker's Handbook*. New York: William Morrow, 1979.

Kirk, Ruth, *The Naturalist's America: Desert, the American Southwest*. Boston: Houghton Mifflin, 1973.

Klots, Alexander B., and Elsie B. Klots, *The Community of Living Things in the Desert*. Mankato, Minn.: Creative Educational Society, 1967.

Kohn, Bernice, *The Beachcomber's Book*. New York: Puffin Books, 1970.

Kruse, Barclay, *How to Select & Use Outdoor Equipment*. Tucson, Ariz.: Fisher Publishing, 1983.

Larson, Peggy, *Deserts of America*. Englewood Cliffs, N.J.: Prentice-Hall, 1970.

Leach, Penelope, *Your Baby & Child: From Birth to Age Five*. New York: Alfred A. Knopf, 1985.

Lippson, Alice Jane, and Robert L. Lippson, *Life in the Chesapeake Bay*. Baltimore, Md.: The Johns Hopkins University Press, 1987.

Mayesky, Mary, Donald Neuman, and Raymond J. Wlodkowski, *Creative Activities for Young Children*. Albany, N.Y.: Delmar, 1985.

Mitchell, Andrew, *The Young Naturalist*. London: Usborne, 1982.

Mitchell, John, and the Massachusetts Audubon Society, *The Curious Naturalist*. Englewood Cliffs, N.J.: Prentice-Hall, 1980.

Musselman, Virginia W., *Learning about Nature through Crafts*. Harrisburg, Pa.: Stackpole, 1969.

Neisser, Edith G., *Primer for Parents of Preschoolers*. New York: Parents' Magazine Press, 1972.

Ranger Rick's NatureScope: Amazing Mammals. 2 parts. Washington, D.C.: National Wildlife Federation, 1986.

Ranger Rick's NatureScope: Discovering Deserts. Washington, D.C.: National Wildlife Federation, 1986.

Ranger Rick's NatureScope: Let's Hear It for Herps! Washington, D.C.: National Wildlife Federation, 1987.

Ranger Rick's NatureScope: Wading into Wetlands. Washington, D.C.: National Wildlife Federation, 1986.

Ranger Rick's NatureScope: Wild about Weather. Washington, D.C.: National Wildlife Federation, 1986.

Redleaf, Rhoda, *Open the Door: Let's Explore*. St. Paul, Minn.: Toys 'n Things Press, 1983.

Ridout, Ronald, and Michael Holt, *The Life Cycle Book of Frogs*. New York: Grosset and Dunlap, 1974.

Riviere, Bill, *The L. L. Bean Guide to the Outdoors*. New York: Random House, 1981.

Rockwell, Robert E., Elizabeth A. Sherwood, and Robert A. Williams, *Hug a Tree: And Other Things to Do Outdoors with Young Children*. Mt. Rainier, Md.: Gryphon House, 1985.

Rosenberg, Stephen N., M.D., *The Johnson & Johnson First Aid Book*. New York: Warner Books, 1985.

Rosengren, John H., *Outdoor Science for the Elementary Grades*. West Nyack, N.Y.: Parker, 1972.

Russell, Helen Ross, *Ten-Minute Field Trips: Using the School Grounds for Environmental Studies*. Chicago: J. G. Ferguson, 1973.

Satterfield, Archie, and Eddie Bauer:
The Eddie Bauer Guide to Backpacking. Reading, Mass.: Addison-Wesley, 1983.
The Eddie Bauer Guide to Family Camping. Reading, Mass.: Addison-Wesley, 1982.

Schickedanz, Judith A., et al., *Strategies for Teaching Young Children*. Englewood Cliffs, N.J.: Prentice-Hall, 1983.

de Schweinitz, Karl, *Growing Up: How We Become Alive, Are Born, and Grow*. New York: The Macmillan Co., 1967.

Shuttlesworth, Dorothy, *Exploring Nature with Your Child*. New York: Plenary Publications International, 1977.

Simon, Hilda, *Wonders of the Butterfly World*. New York: Dodd, Mead, 1963.

Simon, Seymour, *Look to the Night Sky*. New York: The Viking Press, 1977.

Spizman, Robyn Freedman, *Lollipop Grapes and Clothespin Critters*. Reading, Mass.: Addison-Wesley, 1985.

Stein, Sara Bonnett, *Making Babies: An Open Family Book for Parents and Children Together*. New York: Walker, 1974.

Tapley, Donald F., M.D., Robert J. Weiss, M.D., and Thomas Q. Morris, M.D., eds., *The Columbia University College of Physicians and Surgeons Complete Home Medical Guide*. New York:

Crown, 1985.

Thomas, Lowell J., and Joy L. Sanderson, *First Aid for Backpackers and Campers: A Practical Guide to Outdoor Emergencies.* New York: Holt, Rinehart and Winston, 1978.

Tilden, Freeman, *Interpreting Our Heritage.* Chapel Hill, N.C.: The University of North Carolina Press, 1967.

Todd, Vivian Edmiston, and Helen Heffernan, *The Years before School: Guiding Preschool Children.* New York: Macmillan, 1977.

Zarchy, Harry, *The Little Hobby Bookshelf: Butterflies and Moths.* Cleveland: The World Publishing Co., 1966.

PERIODICALS

Carney, Cynthia L., "Family Camping." *Parents,* July 1984.

Carter, Tom, "Taking Baby along for the Ride."

Consumers' Research, August 1985.

Chase, Jim:
"The Family Way." *Backpacker,* July 1985.
"Kids' Stuff." *Backpacker,* July 1985.

Edwards, J. W., "Let Your Kids Take You Camping." *Backpacker,* July 1986.

Miller, Charles A., "Family-Sized Gear for Camping in Comfort." *Popular Science,* May 1984.

Price, Steve, "It's Never Too Soon." *Field & Stream,* May 1986.

Silverman, Goldie, "Backpacking with Babies and Small Children." *Baby Talk,* June 1987.

Van Lear, Denise, "Taking the Worry out of Water." *Backpacker,* July 1985.

PAMPHLETS

"Firemanship." Irving, Texas: Boy Scouts of America, 1982.

"Make Campfires Safe!" Washington D.C.: Forest Service, U.S. Department of Agriculture, November 1980.

"The National Parks: Index 1988." Washington, D.C.: Office of Public Affairs, National Park Service, U.S. Department of the Interior, 1988.

"Safe Food to Go: A Guide to Packing Lunches, Picnicking & Camping Out." Home & Garden Bulletin No. 242. Washington, D.C.: Food Safety and Inspection Service, U.S. Department of Agriculture, May 1986.

"Teaching Your Children about Sexuality." Washington, D.C.: The American College of Obstetricians and Gynecologists, August 1983.

"Type V Hybrid PFDs." Coast Guard Consumer Fact Sheet #15. Washington, D.C.: U.S. Coast Guard, April 1986.

"Your Personal Flotation Device." Chicago: National Safety Council, no date.

Acknowledgments and Picture Credits

The editors wish to thank: Jim Chase, Chappaqua, N.Y.; Mark Farmer, Alexandria, Va.; Jay Humphries, Forest Service, U.S. Department of Agriculture, Washington, D.C.; Celeste Lenzini, Alexandria, Va.; Carol Madeheim, Arizona-Sonora Desert Museum, Tucson, Ariz.; Judith K. Norgaard, Forest Service, U.S. Department of Agriculture, Washington, D.C.; Judy Wester, Framingham, Mass.

Index

Pollen, *86*
Pond:
    dipping, *90-91*
    exploring, *88-91*
Preservation of wilderness, importance of, 63, 68, 79
Preserving:
    butterflies, *104-105*
    dried leaves and flowers, *106-107*
Print:
    fish, *98*
    leaf, *81*

Q

Questions commonly asked:
    about nature, 61
    about sex, 41
Quill pen, making, *55*

R

Rabies, 135
Rainbow, simulating, *35*
Recreational vehicles, renting, 122, 139
Reproduction, 40-41, *42-47*
Reptiles, 71
Rocks:
    collecting, *108*
    cracking open, *101*
Rodents, as pets, 12
Rooting medium, *16*
Rowboat, fishing from, 131, 133
Rubbings:
    of leaves, *81*
    of tree bark, *25*

S

Safety tips, 134-135
Salt evaporation experiment, *95*
Sand painting, *101*
Science experiments:
    with plants, *17*
    precipitation, 32
    salt evaporation, *95*
    with snow and ice, *34*
Scrapbook:
    of tree in seasons, 25
    of zoo visit, *51*
Sea glass, collection of, *109*
Seashore:
    exploring, *94*
    projects, *95-99*
Seasons:
    celebrating rituals of, 74-75
    experiencing at nature centers, 61-62
Seedlings, transplanting, 20

Seeds, *14*
    collecting, 57
    dispersal of, *26*, 85
    growing in sponge garden, *14*
    sowing in ground, 20
    sprouting on socks, 85
Senses:
    of animals, 11
    using to observe, 9
Sex education, 40-41
    birth stories, *42-47*
Sexuality, how to talk about, 41
Skeleton, reassembling of animal, *83*
Skiing equipment, cross-country, 121
Sky, observations of, *36-39*
Sleeping bags, *115*
    arranging in tent, *128*
Snakebites, treating, 134, 136
Snakes:
    handling, *84*
    poisonous, *chart* 136-137
    in terrarium, *92*
Snow:
    experiments with, *34*
    maple candy, 74
Soil, preparing for garden, 19
Solar system, 36
Spider bites, treating, 134, 137
Spiders, 24
Sponge garden, *14*
Spores, mold, *17*
Spring rituals, 75
Sprouting seeds:
    on socks, 85
    in sponge garden, *14*
Stars, in constellations, 36, *38, 39*
Stem cuttings, *16*
Stoves, camp, *126-128*
Stream, exploring, *88-91*
Summer rituals, 75
Sun, relationship of, to earth, *36*
Survival kit, for camping trip, 112
Swamp, 88
Sweet potato vine, sprouting, *16*

T

Tadpoles, *91*
Telescopes:
    for stargazing, *38*
    toy, *28*
Tents:
    choosing and testing, *114*
    sleeping arrangements in, 128
Terrariums, *92*
Thermal injury, 134-135

Thunderstorms, 32
Ticks, 137
Tides, 94
Toads, in terrarium, *92*
Tracks, animal:
    casting, *96*
    of desert animals, *102-103*
    identifying, *82*
Transplants, 20
Traps:
    for gypsy moth, *29*
    for nocturnal insects, *29*
Trees:
    adopting, *25*
    identifying by bark, *25*
    planting at child's birth, 74
Tropical fish, 13
Turtles, *92, 93*

U

Umbrella, for catching insects, *28*

V

Vegetable garden, planning, 19

W

Water, purifying, *125*
Water cycle, *33*
Water safety, *130-132*
Water scope, making, *89*
Water trips, *130-133*
Weather observations, *32-35*
Weather chart, *32*
Weather station, 32
Weather vane, *35*
Web of life, 78-79, 80
Wetlands, expeditions to, *88-91, 93*
Wilderness conservation organizations, 139
Wilderness expeditions:
    to desert, *100-103*
    to fields and woodlands, *80-87*
    to freshwater habitats, *88-91, 93*
    rules for, 78
    to seashore, *94-99*
    to wetlands, *88-91, 93*
    See also Backpacking; Bicycling; Camping; Canoeing; Hiking; Water trips
Winter bug hunt, *29*
Winter rituals, 74-75
Winter solstice, 74
Woodlands, excursions to, *80-87*
Wormery, *21*

Z

Zoo, visiting, 68, *69-70*, 71

Time-Life Books Inc. offers a wide range of fine recordings, including a *Rock 'n' Roll Era* series. For subscription information, call 1-800-621-7026, or write Time-Life Music, P.O. Box C-32068, Richmond, Virginia 23261-2068.